Maxims and Considerations of Chamfort

Translated with an Introduction
by
E. Powys Mathers

Translation first published in two volumes in 1926.

ISBN: 978-1-954357-36-5

INTRODUCTION

Sebastien Roch Nicolas de Chamfort was born near Clermont in the Auvergne in 1741. He was an illegitimate child, and, though it has been supposed that his father was a canon of the Sainte-Chapelle, his only certain possession was the baptismal name of Nicolas; the rest he added for himself.

He won a bursary at the College des Grassins in Paris, and, in the course of his education there, worked brilliantly. As soon as he left, he began to support himself by miscellaneous writing, which is said to have included the composition of sermons at a louis a time; but he had reached the age of twenty-eight before his *Eloge de Molière* won the prize of the Academy, established his literary reputation, and gave him entry into the higher intellectual circles of Paris.

At this time he is spoken of as a man with quite exceptional good looks and bodily strength—*Hercule sous la figure d' Adonis*, Madame de Craon called him—and as one who keenly appreciated the luxuries to which he had attained, and the admiring contact of women. A disease which he caught in the early months of his success, however, remained with him till he died, and his brooding upon it and upon his bastardy obviously influenced his observation towards the dark.

The three further periods of Chamfort's activity before the Revolution can be sketched in a few words.

Madame Helvétius, who had done the same for many another young philosopher, gave him free quarters at Sèvres; and Chabanon, a worthless writer but warm-hearted patron, bestowed a pension upon him which guaranteed him from all future want. He was elected to the Academy, given a further pension by the King, and became Secretary to the Prince de Condé.

But he soon found that this post did not suit him, and appears to have retired somewhat suddenly into a life of seclusion at Auteuil. There he fell in love with a clever and entertaining woman attached to the household of the Duchesse du Maine. The two were married, and six months later Madame de Chamfort was dead.

He returned to Paris, and became Secretary to Madame Elisabeth, the King's sister. This position he retained until an unfortunate love affair caused him to abandon Court for the last time, and seek retirement in the house of his staunch friend Monsieur de Vaudreuil.

Chamfort had, as we have seen, started from nowhere, and there is not a trace of genius in his plays, poems, or Academic essays; yet he had gone anywhere he wished, for his talisman was conversation. This was not of an obviously ingratiating kind, but it served him better than any flattery. From the first he walked through intrigue, pretension, flunkeyism, and despotic arrogance, and, by blasting these qualities with his tongue, became a personage among their exponents. He said things which made all future friendship impossible, and hosts of friends sprang up about him. The Rights of Man was perhaps his most successful paradox.

One of the minor shocks, then, which assailed the Court on the outbreak of the Revolution was the discovery that Chamfort had, in reality, always meant what he said. He cast himself with fervour into the movement, devoted his money and his pen to popular propaganda, and was one of the first of the storming party to enter the Bastille. He took a large part in the new and busy journalism which was born to argue out the National situation, worked with his friend and biographer Ginguené on the *Feuille Villageoise,* wrote for the *Mercure de France,* and composed his *Adresse au Peuple Français* for Talleyrand.

But Chamfort's bitterly critical temper soon involved him in a series of quarrels, and led him inevitably to prefer the unpopular side, even in the popular movement; it was only after their fortunes had begun to decline, for instance, that he consented to become Secretary of the Jacobins. His uncompromising sense of balance betrayed him into such comments as: "Be my brother or I will kill you," and "The Revolution is like a lost dog that nobody dares to stop," which were infinitely less palatable to zealous extremists with no time for a sense of humour, than had been his early denunciations to the leisured agnostics of the old régime.

The ascendancy of Marat and Robespierre sent him definitely into revolt against the Revolution, and, with the fall of the Girondins, his political activity ceased altogether. But he still went on talking, and this brought him, in the end, to one of the strangest deaths in history.

After much hesitation he accepted a half share of the Chief Librarianship of the Bibliothèque Nationale, and, while fulfilling his duties there, was arrested, with four others, on the information of an assistant. The charge against the prisoners seems to have been merely that they spoke in private against the Convention, and they were released from the squalid Madelonettes after a few days, but were compelled to live with a guard in attendance, pending a decision on their case. Chamfort had conceived a profound horror of his prison, and swore that he would rather die than return to it; when, therefore, the guard, after some weeks, abruptly told his charges that they were to be taken back to gaol, and must prepare their bundles, Chamfort retired to his cabinet and made four separate attempts on his life.

He shot himself in the head, the pistol bullet breaking his nose and lodging in his right eye; he cut his throat across several times with a razor, and then tried to reach his heart with the same weapon; finally he was in process of opening his veins when a groan escaped him and he was interrupted.

To those who had come to arrest him, he dictated this statement and signed it firmly in his own blood: "I, Sebastien-Roch-Nicolas-Chamfort, declare that I wanted to die a free man rather than be taken back as a slave to a prison." And then, "You see," he said to Ginguené, "what comes of being clumsy with one's hands."

It is usually said that Chamfort lingered on after his suicide, but as a matter of fact he did more than this; he became well enough to leave his bed, and even found strength to visit his friends and discuss the possibility of resuming journalistic work. His injuries were such, however, that even his abnormal physique could not survive them, and he died on the 13th of April, 1794.

"I am finally leaving," he said, "this world where the heart must be broken or bronzed."

★ ★ ★

It has been already suggested that the bulk of Chamfort's works are valueless; but respecting his *Maxims and Considerations*, the whole of which are here translated into English for the first time, and his *Anecdotes*, masterly pen miniatures of Parisian society, there has been, from very various quarters, a chorus of perhaps not sufficiently critical praise.

Balzac, John Stuart Mill, and Schopenhauer could find no fault with the *Maxims*, and Sainte-Beuve speaks of them as "sharp arrows that arrive suddenly and continue to whistle." Professor Saintsbury says that "they hardly admit a rival," and of their author that "for a kind of tragi-comic satire, a *sæva indignatio* … he has no equal in literature except Swift."

Many of Chamfort's utterances are, indeed, among the sharpest and bitterest ever penned; but they have one general fault: that, when compared with the work in the same kind of such writers as La

Bruyère and La Rochefoucauld, they betray a most noticeable sameness. The sharp, clean, personal outline which has been so praised in Chamfort's style is, in fact and frequently, present; but the image is so identical that it gives an effect of mechanical reproduction. It would not perhaps be too fanciful to say that La Rochefoucauld used his pen as a pen, La Bruyère his as a paintbrush, and Chamfort his as a steel embossing stamp. And there are three or four particular faults that it is necessary, in fairness, to enumerate in conjunction with this more general one; for it may be possible to show that all arose out of the tragedy of Chamfort's death, and would not have remained if he had lived to prepare his shorter writings for the public.

A careful reader of the maxims cannot fail to be struck by the following defects: that Chamfort sometimes exasperatingly draws out a good story until it is spoilt, talcing ten lines to obscure a tale which would have shone brilliantly in two; that he will do the same with a simple thought, and worry it till it has lost its force; that he will quite often start with one thought, half work it out, and then slip away from it to another, (his epigram, in other words, is often either an *essay*, or a confusion of two thoughts which have occurred to the author simultaneously) ; that he will occasionally get into a tangle with his prose, and be definitely ungrammatical; and that he will sometimes, in spite of his great range of reading, fail to verify some illustration, and so use it incorrectly.

All critics, favourable and adverse, seem to have judged the *Maxims and Considerations* as if they were finished work; and yet the story of the condition and purpose of their collection quite clearly proves that they were not. Ginguené, who was their contemporary editor, tells us that it had always been Chamfort's habit to jot down his thoughts on little squares of paper and to stow these papers, perhaps with scarcely a second glance, into portfolios. But between the time of Chamfort's death and the coming of the Juge de Paix, all these containers, he says, had been emptied, and the large majority of their contents destroyed. The chance selection of notes remaining formed the sole material from which the two volumes, of *Maxims* and of *Anecdotes*, were ultimately taken; and with them Ginguené discovered a sketch for a greater work, *Produits de la Civilisation Perfectionnée*, of which they were to have formed the basis. When we consider, then, that we have only the unweeded, unrevised, haphazard moiety of Chamfort's work in his most personal manner, it is surely not too much to suppose that, if the *Produits* had been allowed to come to a natural birth, its contents would have shown a flexibility, economy, variety, and exactness which might, in combination with the colour and audacity and passion surviving in the rough notes, have set its author very high indeed.

Chamfort was utterly lacking in self interest, and he even fought consistently against his own advantage. He attacked and destroyed the pensions and institutions which were vital to his body, and also, because he esteemed it to be false, the school of literary wit which fed the pride of his spirit.

If the whole secret of his character is to be found in any one sentence of his, then it is to be found in this: "Any man who is not a misanthrope at forty has never loved mankind." He only hated men, it has been said, because they would not love themselves.

In 1783 Chamfort met Mirabeau, and the two remained on terms of intimate friendship until the latter's death in 1791. Their relation was definitely that of master and pupil, and Mirabeau would go humbly to pass an hour with Chamfort nearly every morning in order, as he said, "to rub the most electric head in France." Never a day passed, he confesses, in which he did not find himself saying: "Chamfort would frown, no, let's not describe that."

"You are living proof that it is not true that you have to bend or break," Mirabeau writes, and again, from London: "O my dear and worthy Chamfort, I feel that in losing you, I lose part of my strength, my arrows have been stolen from me."

CHAPTER I.

GENERAL MAXIMS

I. Maxims, axioms and epitomes are the work of intellectual men, who have made them, it would seem, for the use of commonplace or idle minds. The lazy man delights in a maxim that spares him from making the same observations which have led its author to his result. The idle and the commonplace person feels himself absolved from going any further, and gives the maxim a general application which the author, unless as sometimes happens he be himself a commonplace person, has never claimed for it. The man of superior intelligence at once seizes upon those resemblances or differences which make the maxim more, or less, or not at all, applicable to such or such a case. It is in this matter as in natural history, where the desire for simplification has created imaginary classes and divisions. It has, indeed, required intelligence to do this, since it has been necessary to collect and study the evidence; but the great naturalist, the man of genius, is he who sees nature prodigal of beings that differ individually, and who recognises the insufficiency of those divisions and classes so helpful to the commonplace or lazy minds which I have mentioned. We can associate these two for they are often one; they are often cause and effect.

II. Most of those who make collections of verse or epigram are like men eating cherries or oysters: they choose out the best at first, and end by eating all.

III. What a curious book it would be that should point out all those ideas which are subversive of the human spirit, of society, and of morals, and which are yet to be found developed or taken for granted in the most celebrated writings, in the most established of authors: ideas which propagate religious superstition, unsound political doctrine, despotism, the vanity of rank, and popular prejudice of every kind. We should see that all books corrupt, and that the best do almost as much harm as good.

IV. Man is always writing about Education, and the works composed on this subject have produced some happy ideas, some useful methods, have, in a word, achieved some partial good. But what can be the ultimate use of such writings when reforms in legislation, religion, and public opinion, do not keep pace with them? Since Education has no other object than to make the reason of childhood conform to public reason in these three matters, what useful instruction can we give as long as the three are mutually at war? When you develop a child's intelligence you are only preparing him to see the absurdity of opinions and customs consecrated by the seal of religious, public, or legislative authority, sooner than he otherwise would, and, consequently, inspiring him with a contempt for these things.

V. To analyse those ideas which enter into the different judgments formed by such and such a man, or such and such a community, both engenders philosophy and is productive of pleasure. To examine the ideas which determine such and such item of public opinion is not less interesting, and is often even more so.

VI. It is in Civilisation as in cookery. When we see light, healthy, well-made dishes on the table, we rejoice because cookery has become a science; but when we see gravies, jellies, and truffle patty, we curse the cooks and their disastrous art: apply this now.

VII. In the present state of Society man seems to me corrupted more by his reason than by his passions. His passions (those, I mean, which also belong to primitive man) have preserved to the social order what little of nature is still to be found there.

VIII. Society is not, as is commonly supposed, the development of Nature, but rather her decomposition and entire recasting. It is a second building made from the ruins of the first; and our pleasure is mingled with surprise when we find unutilised fragments. The artless expression of a natural feeling, escaping in Society, rouses this emotion in us; and it even happens that we are more pleased if it proceeds from one of higher rank, that is to say, one further away from Nature. It charms us in a King, because a king is at the opposite extremity. It is a fragment of ancient Gothic or Corinthian architecture discovered in an ugly modern building.

IX. Generally speaking, if Society were not an artificial composition, each true and simple feeling would not affect it so considerably. It would please, without astonishing us; but, in fact, it both astonishes and pleases. Our surprise is a satire on Society, our pleasure an homage to Nature.

X. Knaves have always a certain need of their honour, somewhat as police spies are paid less when they move in less good company.

XI. A man of the people, a beggar, may allow himself to be slighted without appearing disgraced, if the slight seem levelled at his exterior condition only. But if the same beggar allows his conscience to be insulted, even by the first Sovereign in Europe, he becomes as base in his own self as in estate.

XII. It must be owned impossible to live in Society without playing a part from time to time. An honest man is distinguished from a rogue by the fact that he only plays it in cases of strict necessity and to escape from danger, while the other goes out of his way to make occasions to do so.

XIII. Folk in Society sometimes use a very strange line of argument. If they wish to reject a man's testimony in favour of another man, they say: he is your friend. But, damn it, it is just because my good report of him is true, just because he is exactly as I describe him, that he *is* my friend. You mistake cause for effect, and effect for cause. Why should you think I speak well of him because he is my friend? Why not rather suppose him to be my friend because I can speak well of him?

XIV. There are two classes of Moralists and Politicians: those, and they are the more numerous, who have only looked at human nature on its odious or ridiculous side: Lucian, Montaigne, La Bruyère, La Rochefoucauld, Swift, Mandeville, Helvetius, and the rest: and those, such as Shaftesbury and a few others, who have only regarded her on the fair side, and seen her perfections. The first know nothing of the palace, because they have only seen its privies. The second are enthusiasts who turn their eyes away from what offends them; but the offence remains. *Est in medio verum.*

XV. Do you want absolute proof of the futility of all books of Ethics, Sermons, and the like? You have only to glance at the prejudice in favour of hereditary position. Is there a single abuse against which Philosophers, Orators, and Poets have launched more satire; which has given birth to more sarcasm; which has more exercised all kinds of wit? Yet have these things done away with presentations, or the fantasy of riding in coaches, or Cherin's office?[1]

XVI. In the Theatre we aim at effect; but the difference between a good and a bad poet is that the former desires to make his effect by reasonable means, while all means seem admirable to the latter.

---

[1] Bernard Cherin, the Genealogist Royal.

It is the same with honest men and rogues, when both would seek their fortune. The first use only honest means; and the second, means of any sort.

XVII. Philosophy, like Medicine, has many drugs, a very few good remedies, and practically no specifics.

XVIII. There are computed to be about a hundred and fifty million souls in Europe, double that amount in Africa, and more than treble in Asia; even admitting that America and the Southern Lands only contain half this number of inhabitants, we can be certain that more than a hundred thousand persons die in the world every day. So that a man who has only lived for thirty years has escaped this tremendous destruction about one thousand, four hundred times.

XIX. I have seen men whose only endowment was a simple and straight-forward reasonableness, with no great breadth and without any considerable eminence of intellect; yet this reasonableness sufficed them for putting all human vanities and absurdities in their place, gave them a sentiment of personal dignity, and enabled them to appreciate the same in others. And I have known women in almost the same case, whose true sensibility, awakened early in life, has lifted them to the same level of idea. It follows from these two observations of mine that those who set a high value on the human vanities and absurdities mentioned above belong to the lowest division of our kind.

XX. He who cannot take refuge in pleasantry at the right moment, and who lacks all pliancy of mind, very often finds himself faced by the necessity of being either deceitful or pedantic: this is an annoying alternative from which a self-respecting man can only extricate himself, in most cases, by charm and humour.

XXI. Often an opinion or custom seems absurd to us in early youth; but as we advance in life we see the reason for it, and it appears less fatuous. Must we conclude from this that certain customs actually are less absurd? One is sometimes led to suppose that they have been established by folk who have read the whole of the book of life, and that they are criticised by those who, in spite of their intelligence, have only read a page or two at best.

XXII. According to the received ideas of society and social fitness, it seems that a priest or parson must believe a little in order not to be a hypocrite, and yet, to avoid intolerance, be not quite sure of his belief. The Grand-Vicar can smile at a remark against religion, the Bishop laugh outright, the Cardinal add a few words of his own.

XXIII. Most nobles recall their ancestors, rather as a *Cicerone* in Italy may recall Cicero.

XXIV. I have read in the works of some traveller that certain African savages believe in the immortality of the soul. Without pretending to explain what becomes of it, they conceive that it wanders after death in the bushes which surround their villages, and they even go out to seek for it on many consecutive mornings. But, not finding it, they abandon their search, and think no more of the matter. This is rather what our philosophers have done, and the best they could do.

XXV. An upright man should achieve public esteem without having thought about it, and, as it were, in spite of himself. He who has sought it shows what it is worth.

XXVI. That Tree, in the Bible, of the Knowledge of Good and Evil which brings forth Death, is an excellent allegory. Does not this symbol mean that when we have penetrated to the root of things, the loss of our illusions brings death upon the soul, that is to say, a complete indifference to all that concerns and busies other men?

XXVII. There needs must be something of everything in the world; even in the artificial combinations of the social system there needs must be men who oppose Nature to Society, truth to opinion, and reality to the accepted thing. This is an attractive kind of intelligence and character, and its sway is felt more often than people suppose. One has but to exhibit the truth to some folk, and they make for it with a simple and appealing air of astonishment. They are surprised that so striking a matter (when one can make it so, that is) could have escaped them until that very minute.

XXVIII. People think that a deaf man is unhappy in Society, but is not this opinion the conceit of

Society herself: it is a terrible deprivation for this man that he cannot hear what we are saying?

XXIX. Thought consoles for all, and is a cure for all. If sometimes she seems to hurt you, ask her for a remedy against that hurt, and she will give it.

XXX. It is impossible to deny that there are some great characters in modern history; and we cannot understand how they appear. They seem out of place. They are like caryatides in the entresol.

XXXI. In dealing with Society the best philosophy is to combine the sarcasm of laughter with the indulgence of contempt.

XXXII. I am no more astonished to see one man wearied by Glory than to see another disturbed by the noise in his anteroom.

XXXIII. I have seen in this world the esteem of honest men continually sacrificed to reputation, rest to celebrity.

XXXIV. According to Dorilas, weighty proof of the existence of God is furnished by the existence of man; of man in perfection, of man in the least equivocal sense of the term, in the most precise and therefore somewhat restricted sense; by the existence, in a word, of the man of quality. There you have the masterpiece of Providence, or rather the only work directly from his hands. But it is claimed, it is affirmed that there are other beings exactly resembling this favoured creature. The same shape, asks Dorilas, the same external conformation? Can this be true ? And so, touching the existence of these individuals, of these men, since people call them so; an existence which he has previously denied but which, to his considerable surprise, he has seen recognised by several of his equals, and which, for this reason alone, he formally denies no longer; of which he is merely suspicious, pardonably and quite involuntarily doubtful, against which he is content simply to protest by arrogance, by forgetting his manners, or by contemptuous kindness; touching, I say, these doubtless ill-defined existences, what is poor Dorilas to do? How shall he explain them? How shall he reconcile this phenomenon with his theory? To what physical, metaphysical, or if necessary mythological system shall he turn for the solution of his problem? Now he reflects and ponders in good earnest; for the objection is plausible and disturbs him. He has intelligence and some learning; he means to find the answer to his riddle; he finds it, he grasps it, and his eyes shine for joy. Silence. In Persian Theology there is a doctrine of two principles, of Good and Evil. Still you do not understand? Yet nothing could be more simple. Genius, talent, and virtue are invented by the Evil principle, by Ahriman, by the Devil, to drag certain poor wretches into the daylight, admitted plebeians, veritable commoners, or, at any rate, scarcely gentlemen.

XXXV. How many distinguished military men, how many gallant officers have died without bequeathing their names to posterity: being in this less fortunate than Bucephalus, or even than Berecillo, the Spanish mastiff, who ate up the Indians at San Domingo and had three soldiers' pay!

XXXVI. We desire the idleness of a wicked man, and the silence of a fool.

XXXVII. The best explanation of why dishonest men and even fools are nearly always more successful in making their way in the world than the upright and intelligent, is that a dishonest man or a fool has little trouble in becoming acquainted with and attuned to the ways of the world; for these, generally speaking, consist only of dishonesty and foolishness. But upright and reasonable men lose time valuable to their undertaking through not being able to get into touch with Society. The first are merchants who sell out and restock immediately, because they know the language of the country; while the second are obliged to learn the speech both of their dealers and of their customers. Often, indeed, they scorn to acquire this language before they display their goods and begin to bargain, and then they are forced to retire without making a single sale.

XXXVIII. There is a prudence better than the quality which we ordinarily call so, the prudence of the eagle as opposed to that of the mole. It consists in resolutely following one's own character, boldly accepting such disadvantages and accidents as it may bring. . . .

XXXIX. We have to consider what man would be without Reason, if we are to succeed in pardoning Reason for the harm it does to the majority of men. It is a necessary evil.

XL. There is such a thing as well-clothed foolishness, just as there are certain very well-dressed fools.

XLI. If Adam had been told, on the day after the death of Abel, that in some hundreds of years there would be places where seven or eight thousand men should collect in a mass together within the compass of four square leagues, would he have believed that these multitudes could ever live at peace? Would he not have imagined even more shocking and monstrous crimes than those which actually occur? This must be our reflection, when we would console ourselves for the abuses inseparable from these astounding agglomerations of men.

XLII. Pretensions are a source of misery, and the happy time of life begins only when they are discarded. If a woman be still lovely when her beauty begins to fade she makes herself either ridiculous or unhappy by her pretensions; but ten years later, when she is older and uglier, she is both serene and untroubled. When a man reaches that age at which he either may or may not be fortunate with women, he lays himself open to annoyance and even to shame; but when he becomes impotent, uncertainty passes and he is at peace. Unstable and indeterminate ideas are the cause of all the mischief. It is better to be something less and that indisputably. The status of dukes and peers, which is well established, is worth more than that of foreign princes who have to struggle unceasingly for their pre-eminence. If Chapelain had followed the course advised by Boileau in the famous half line *Why does he not write in prose?* he would have spared himself much vexation, and perhaps made a name for himself other than as a laughing-stock.

XLIII. Seneca said to one of his sons, who could not compass the exordium of a speech on which he had embarked: Are you not ashamed to wish to speak better than you can? In the same way, one might say to those who embrace principles stronger than their character: Are you not ashamed to wish to be more of a philosopher than you can be?

XLIV. The majority of those who inhabit the world live there so heedlessly and think so little, that they know nothing of it though it lies ever beneath their eyes. They do not know it, M. de B... used pleasantly to remark, for the same reason that cockchafers are ignorant of natural history.

XLV. When we see Bacon, at the beginning of the sixteenth century, point out to human genius the way it must take to rebuild the house of the Sciences, we almost cease to admire the great men who have come after him, such as Boyle and Locke. He parcels out for them in advance the territories which they have to clear or subjugate. Caesar, now master of the world after the victory of Pharsalia, is giving kingdoms and provinces to his supporters or his favourites.

XLVI. Our Reason sometimes makes us as unhappy as our passions may; and we can say of a man, when this is so, that he is a patient poisoned by his doctor.

XLVII. We often regret the moment when we lose our illusions and the passions of our youth; but sometimes we hate the spell which has deceived us. This is Armida burning and destroying the palace wherein she was enchanted.

XLVIII. Doctors and laymen are equally in the dark concerning the diseases and interior of the human body. They are all blind, but doctors are the Quinze-Vingts[2] who know the roads better and evade their difficulties more easily.

XLIX. Do you want to know how people make their fortunes? Observe what happens in the pit of a theatre on a crowded day, see how some remain at the back, how those in front are pulled to the rear, and how those behind are carried forward. This illustration is so apt that it has passed into common speech. They call making one's fortune, *pushing oneself to the front. My son, my nephew will push himself to the front.* Respectable people speak of *advancing,* of *making progress,* of *attaining:* softened phrases which

---

[2] Inmates of the Quinze-Vingts, an asylum in Paris for three hundred blind men.

gloss over the accessory idea of force, violence, and coarseness, but leave the principal idea unchanged.

L. The physical World seems to be the work of a powerful and well-intentioned Being, who was obliged to leave the execution of a part of his plan to some malignant Power. But the moral World would seem to be born of the caprices of a devil gone mad.

LI. Those who only give their word as authority for an assertion the whole force of which depends upon proof, are like the man who said: I have the honour to inform you that the earth moves round the sun.

LII. In great matters men show themselves as they ought; in little, as they are.

LIII. What is a Philosopher? A man who sets Nature against Law, reason against custom, conscience against opinion, and judgment against error.

LIV. A fool who has a moment's flash of wit is both astonishing and shocking, like cab horses at a gallop.

LV. To be in no one's hand, to be *one's own man* in heart and principle and feeling … that is the rarest thing that I have ever seen.

LVI. Instead of trying to punish men for faults which are intolerable to Society, we ought to punish the weakness of those who bear with them.

LVII. Three-quarters of folly is but foolishness.

LVIII. Because folly is the queen of fools, opinion is queen of the world.

LIX. We must know how to commit such foolishness as our character demands.

LX. Eminence without merit earns deference without esteem.

LXI. Say what you will, both great and small should tell each other, as the coachman told the courtesans in *Le Moulin de Javelle*: "Your kind and my kind can't do without each others' kind."

LXII. Someone said that Providence was the Christian name of chance: a godly person will say that chance is a nickname for Providence.

LXIII. Few men allow themselves to make strong and courageous use of their reason, or dare to apply it in full force to all things equally. The time has come when reason, in such fulness, must be brought to bear on every Moral, Political, or Social aim, on kings and ministers, on the great of the earth, on philosophers, and on all the principles of Science and the Fine Arts. Otherwise we shall remain in a state of mediocrity.

LXIV. There are men who must excel, who must lift themselves above their fellows at any price whatever. It is all one to them, provided they can be conspicuous on some mountebank elevation;

theatre, throne, or scaffold suits them equally, as long as the eyes of men are upon them.

LXV. Men grow little by being massed together; they are Milton's devils, who had to become dwarfs to enter Pandemonium.

LXVI. We stultify our real character for fear of being looked at and attracting attention; we bury ourselves in nonentity to escape the peril of being talked about.

LXVII. The physical plagues and misfortunes of human nature have made Society necessary. Society has added to the ills of Nature. The difficulties of Society have created the necessity for Government, and Government now adds to the evils of Society. There you have the history of man.

LXVIII. Ambition takes hold of little souls more easily than great, just as fire catches the straw of a thatched cottage more quickly than a palace.

LXIX. Man lives much with himself and then he has need of virtue; when he lives with others, he has need of honour.

LXX. The fable of Tantalus is hardly ever applied except to the passion of avarice; but it is at least as applicable to ambition, to the love of glory, and to nearly all the other passions.

LXXI. It seems as if Nature, when she gave birth to reason and the passions, wished with her second gift to deaden for man the evils arising from her first; and, in letting him live only a few years after he has lost his passions, she appears to pity him, for she frees him from a life in which reason would be his one resource.

LXXII. All passions exaggerate; it is only because they exaggerate that they are passions.

LXXIII. A philosopher trying to extinguish his passions is like an alchemist putting out his fire.

LXXIV. The chief of Nature's gifts is that power of reason which lifts us above our passions and weaknesses, and even enables us to control our talents, virtues, and good qualities.

LXXV. Why are men so foolish, so ridden by custom or by the fear of making a will, why, in a word, are they so imbecile as to leave their goods to those who will laugh at their dying, rather than to those who will weep when they are dead?

LXXVI. Nature meant there to be illusions for the wise as well as the foolish, so that the wise should not be made too unhappy by their wisdom.

LXXVII. To see the way in which the sick are treated in hospitals one would suppose that man had invented these sorry asylums, not to cure the diseased but to remove them from the sight of the well and happy, whose enjoyment they are apt to spoil.

LXXVIII. In our days those who love Nature are accused of being romantic.

LXXIX. There is one great objection to the tragic Drama, it attaches too much importance to life and death.

LXXX. Of all days, the day on which one has not laughed is the one most surely wasted.

LXXXI. The majority of follies are born of foolishness.

LXXXII. We pervert our intelligence, conscience, or reason, in the same way as we spoil our stomachs.

LXXXIII. Secrets and deposits are governed by the same law.

LXXXIV. The mind is often to the heart only what the library of a country house is to its owner.

LXXXV. The things which poets, orators, and even a few philosophers tell us about the love of Glory, are exactly the things we are told at College to encourage us to win prizes. And what they say to children to make them prefer the praise of their nurses to a tartlet, they repeat to grown men to make them prefer the eulogy of their fellows or of posterity to personal advantage.

LXXXVI. If you wish to become a Philosopher you must not be disheartened by the first distressing discoveries you make in your study of human beings. To learn these thoroughly you must triumph over the dissatisfactions they afford you, as an anatomist triumphs over Nature and his bodily disgust in order to become proficient in his calling.

LXXXVII. We learn to despise death in the process of becoming acquainted with the evils of Nature; but in becoming acquainted with the evils of Society we learn to despise life.

LXXXVIII. The worth of men is like the worth of diamonds; for these stones have a sure and determined value up to a certain degree of greatness, purity, and perfection, but, above that, are of no fixed value and find no buyers.

CHAPTER II.

FURTHER GENERAL MAXIMS

LXXXIX. In France everyone appears witty, and the reason for this is simple enough. Since everything there is a series of contradictions, the most cursory observation is sufficient to bring the two terms of a contradiction to one's notice, and then to isolate them in one's mind. Legitimate contrasts inevitably follow and these make the man who thinks of them appear to possess a very pretty wit. The art of storytelling is extravagance. A simple newsmonger becomes a first rate wag, just as the historian will, some day, seem a satirist.

XC. The Public does not believe at all in the purity of certain virtues and feelings; speaking generally, the Public can only raise itself to the height of low ideas.

XCI. No man can be, by himself, as despicable as a body of men; and no body of men can be as despicable as the Public.

XCII. There are certain centuries in which public opinion is the worst of all opinions.

XCIII. Hope is a mountebank who ever cheats us, and I for one never knew happiness until I had lost all hope. I would gladly inscribe on the gates of Heaven those words which Dante set upon the gates of Hell: *Lasciate ogni speranza, voi ch'entrate.*

XCIV. A poor yet independent man is only at the disposition of necessity; but a rich, dependent man is at the beck and call of his own kind, either one or many.

XCV. An ambitious man who has missed his goal and lives on in despair, reminds me of Ixion chained to the wheel for having loved a cloud.

XCVI. There is the same difference between an evil and witty man and a good honest wit, as there is between an assassin and a gentleman who fences well.

XCVII. What good is it to appear to have fewer weaknesses than another, and thus to give men fewer holds upon one? A single weakness is fatal if it become known. One should be Achilles *without his heel*, and that would seem to be impossible.

XCVIII. So wretched is the state of man that he must seek in Society his consolation for the evils of Nature, and in Nature his consolation for the evils of Society. And how many men have failed to find consolation in either!

XCIX. Take the most unjust and, in point of interest, the most nonsensical claim you will, one which would be contemptuously dismissed by any company of honest men chosen to arbitrate upon it, and make it the crux of a lawsuit in the regular courts. Any legal case may win or lose; the odds are equal, for or against. Again, take the most ridiculous opinion or statement, and make it the subject of a debate between opposing parties at a meeting of any society; it may quite possibly win by a majority of votes.

C. It is an admitted truth that our age has re-established the meaning of words, that it has, by banishing scholastic, dialectical, and metaphysical subtleties, returned to simplicity and truth in politics, ethics, and natural philosophy. To take the case of ethics alone, we know how many complex and metaphysical ideas were comprehended in the word *honour.* Our age has felt the disadvantage of this, and, to restore complete simplicity, to guard against all possible abuse of words, it has laid down that any man who has not been a convict retains his *honour* in its entirety. Formerly this word was a source of ambiguity and dispute; but now nothing can be clearer. Has a man been in the pillory or has he not, that is the question. It is a simple matter of fact which can be easily determined by reference to the registers in the clerk's office. If a man has not been in the pillory, he is a man of honour who can aspire to anything, to office in the ministry, or what you will. He has the right of entry into corporations, academies, and the courts of kings. We cannot fail to observe how this clarity and precision saves all wrangling or dispute, and how easy and agreeable social intercourse becomes.

CI. So the love of Glory is a virtue! But it is a strange virtue surely that prospers by the action of all the vices, that receives its stimulus from pride, ambition, envy, vanity, and sometimes even from avarice! Would Titus have been Titus, with Sejanus, Narcissus, and Tigelinus as his ministers?

CII. Glory often puts an honest man to the same ordeal as Fortune; that is to say, before either will let him achieve her, she obliges him to do or submit to things unworthy of his character. The bravely virtuous man repels them both, and hides himself in obscurity, or misfortune, or the two together.

CIII. The man exactly situated between our enemy and ourselves, seems nearer to our enemy. This is the result of that optical law which makes a fountain jet appear less distant from the far side of the basin than from the side on which we stand.

CIV. Public opinion is a bar of judgment at which the honest man should never refuse to plead, but the jurisdiction of which he should never entirely acknowledge.

CV. Vain means empty, and thus, though vanity is such a wretched thing, you can scarcely find anything worse to call it than its name. Its name proclaims it for what it is.

CVI. It is commonly supposed that the art of pleasing is a wonderful aid in the pursuit of fortune; but the art of being bored is infinitely more successful. A genius for fortune-hunting, like a genius for succeeding with women, reduces itself almost entirely to this one accomplishment.

CVII. There are few men of high character who have not something of the romantic either in head or heart. The man who altogether lacks this quality, however great his honesty and intelligence may be, compares with the lofty character as an extremely able artist with no ideal of perfection compares with a man of genius whose thought is ever on familiar terms with the perfect beauty.

CVIII. There are some men whose virtue shines more brightly in private than in public life. Her frame disfigures her. The finer a diamond, the lighter should be its setting; the richer the bezel, the poorer appears the stone.

CIX. To avoid quackery avoid the public platform, for once you are mounted there you have either to be a charlatan or have stones thrown at you by the people.

CX. There are few vices as likely to diminish the number of a man's friends, as can an excessive possession of fine qualities.

CXI. There is a kind of superiority or pretension which not to recognise destroys, and another sort which not to perceive makes ineffective.

CXII. To be able to distinguish all the points at which pride differs from vanity is to be far advanced in the study of Ethics. Pride is lofty, calm, intrepid, serene and unshakeable; vanity is worthless and undecided, fickle, restless and irresolute. Pride makes a man greater, but vanity swells him. A thousand virtues spring from pride, nearly all vices and defects are born of vanity. There is a sort of pride which comprehends every commandment of God, and a kind of vanity which, in itself, embraces the seven deadly sins.

CXIII. Life is a disease from which sleep gives us alleviation every sixteen hours. Sleep is a palliative, Death is the remedy.

CXIV. Nature seems to employ men in the furtherance of her designs without being in the least concerned for her instruments: tyrants get rid of those whom they have used.

CXV. There are two things to which we must become inured on pain of finding life intolerable: the outrages of time and man's injustice.

CXVI. I cannot conceive of a wisdom without diffidence. The Scriptures say that the beginning of wisdom is the fear of God, but I believe it is the fear of man.

CXVII. There are certain faults which preserve us from certain epidemic vices: in times of plague those who are ill of quartan fever are seen to escape contagion.

CXVIII. The great evil of the passions does not lie in the torments which they bring upon men, but in the faults and shameful actions they cause him to commit. Were it not for this drawback they would have too great an advantage over cold reason, which can never be productive of happiness. His passions make man *live,* his wisdom only makes him *last.*

CXIX. A man without nobility cannot have kindliness; he can only have good nature.

CXX. One should be able to associate opposites, a love of virtue with an indifference to public opinion, a taste for work with an indifference to glory, and a care for one's health with an indifference to living.

CXXI. The man who cures the thirst of a dropsical person does better than the man who gives him a barrel of wine. Apply this thought to riches.

CXXII. Wicked people sometimes perform good actions. I suppose they wish to see if this gives as great a feeling of pleasure as the virtuous claim for it.

CXXIII. If Diogenes lived in our time his lantern would have to be a dark lantern.

CXXIV. It must be admitted that there are some parts of the soul which we must entirely *paralyse* before we can live happily in this world.

CXXV. Fortune and her trappings turn life into a stage play, where, in the long run, the most upright man becomes the funny man in spite of himself.

CXXVI. Each thing among things is *composite*, each man among men is *patchwork.* Whether on the moral or physical plane, all things are compound. Nothing is one thing only, nothing is pure.

CXXVII. If the painful truths, regrettable discoveries, and Society secrets, which make up the knowledge of a man of the world at forty, had been known to the same man when he was twenty, he would either have fallen into despair or deliberately undertaken his own corruption; and yet we meet a few judicious persons who have reached this age, clear-sighted and well-informed on all these matters, and nevertheless are neither corrupt nor miserable. Discretion steers their virtue through the public depravity, and strength of character combined with the insight of a far-reaching intelligence, lifts them above that disappointment which the perversity of man is likely to engender.

CXXVIII. If you would find to what extent each condition of Society can corrupt a man, examine what he is when he has undergone that influence for the longest possible time, that is to say, when he is old. See what an old courtier is like, an old priest, an old judge, an old solicitor, an old surgeon.

CXXIX. A man without principles is generally also a man without character, for, if he had been born with character, he would have felt the need of creating principles for himself.

CXXX. It is safe to wager that every public idea and every accepted convention is sheer foolishness, because it has suited the majority.

CXXXI. Esteem is better than celebrity, respect is better than renown, and honour than glory.

CXXXII. Vanity is often the impulse which drives man to put forth the full energy of his soul. Wood added to pointed steel will make a dart; two feathers added to the wood will make an arrow.

CXXXIII. Weak men are the light troops in the army of the wicked. They do more harm than the main force; they overrun and ravage the country.

CXXXIV. Some things are easier to legalise than to legitimate.

CXXXV. Celebrity: the advantage of being known by those who do not know you.

CXXXVI. We gladly share in our friends' friendship for people who do not particularly interest us; but even the most perfectly justified hate can hardly get itself respected.

CXXXVII. Many a man has been feared for his talents and hated for his virtues; only his character has at last restored confidence in him. And how long it was before he received this justice!

CXXXVIII. In the natural, as in the social order, we ought not to wish to be more than we can be.

CXXXIX. Folly would not be altogether folly if it were not afraid of wit. Vice would not be altogether vice if it did not hate virtue.

CXL. It is not true (as Rousseau has followed Plutarch in saying) that the more one thinks, the less one feels; but it is true that the more one judges the less one loves. Very few men oblige us to make an exception to this rule.

CXLI. Those who refer everything to the opinion of others are like comedians who act badly, when the public taste is bad, in order to be applauded. Some of them could have acted well if the taste of the audience had been good. An upright man plays his part as excellently as he can, with no thought for the gallery.

CXLII. There is a kind of pleasure in the courage which rises superior to fortune. To despise money is to dethrone a King. There is a zest in this.

CXLIII. There is a sort of indulgence towards one's enemies which is manifest foolishness, rather than kindness or magnanimity. M. de C… appears to me ridiculous because of this tendency in him. He is like Harlequin, who says: *You have smacked my face but I am not at all angry yet.* One should have spirit enough to hate one's enemies.

CXLIV. Though Robinson was destitute and driven to the hardest sorts of labour to secure his daily bread upon his island, he managed to support life and even experienced, on his own confession, several periods of happiness. If he had been cast on an enchanted isle, replete with all that makes existence pleasant, it is possible that lack of employment might have rendered his life quite insupportable.

CXLV. Man's ideas are like card and other games. Ideas which I once heard stigmatised as dangerous and over-daring have since become common and even trivial, and have sunk to be the tenets of quite unworthy persons. Some ideas which we call audacious nowadays will seem feeble and ordinary to our descendants.

CXLVI. I have often noticed in my reading that the first impulse of those who have done an heroic action, who have let themselves yield to a generous impulse, who have rescued their fellows from misfortune, who have run some terrible risk and thereby purchased great benefit for others or for the race … I have, I repeat, noticed that their first impulse is to refuse whatever reward is offered them. This feeling may be found in the poorest and lowest of the people; and we cannot but wonder at a moral instinct which teaches an uneducated man that the reward of such actions is in the heart of their performer. It seems as if paid heroism were nullified.

CXLVII. A virtuous act, a sacrifice either of his interests or of himself, is a matter of necessity to a noble spirit, to a generous temperament a matter of self-respect, and even, in some sort, the egoism of a lofty character.

CXLVIII. Concord between brothers is so rare that Fable only tells us of one couple who were friends, and these, she says, never set eyes on each other, since they passed, turn and turn about, from earth to the Elysian Fields: a circumstance which prevented any occasion of dispute or cleavage.

CXLIX. There are more fools than wise men, and even in a wise man there is more folly than wisdom.

CL. In the conduct of life general Maxims take that place which rules of thumb take in the Arts.

CLI. Conviction is the conscience of intellect.

CLII. Happiness or unhappiness spring from a multitude of causes which never appear, of which we do not speak, of which we could not speak.

CLIII. Pleasure may rest upon illusion, but felicity must repose on truth. Truth alone can give us all of which human nature is capable. The income of a man whose happiness is in illusion may be said to be dependent on the stock market, but a man whose happiness is based on truth has his fortune in landed property, and well secured at that.

CLIV. There are very few things in the world on which an upright man can pasture his soul or his thought agreeably.

CLV. When I hear it contended that the least sensitive are, on the whole, the most happy, I recall that Indian proverb: *It is better to sit down than to stand, it is better to lie down than to sit, but death is the best of all.*

CLVI. Capacity stands in the same relation to cunning as dexterity does to pocket-picking.

CLVII. Obstinacy is a sign of *character* if an amorous disposition is a sign of *love.*

CLVIII. Love, a pleasant folly; ambition, a serious stupidity.

CLIX. Prejudice, vanity, and calculation govern the world; and the man who regulates his conduct by reason, feeling, and truth, has practically nothing in common with Society. He must seek and find nearly all his happiness within himself.

CLX. We must be just before we are generous; we need shirts before ruffles.

CLXI. The Dutch have no pity to spare for debtors. They think that a man in debt lives at the expense of his fellow citizens if he is poor, and at the expense of his heirs if he is rich.

CLXII. Fortune is often like those wealthy and extravagant women who ruin the houses to which they brought rich marriage-portions.

CLXIII. Change of fashion is the tax levied by the industry of the poor on the vanity of the rich.

CLXIV. Preoccupation with money is the great test of small natures, but only a small test of great ones; there may be a wide gulf between a man who despises money and a genuinely honest man.

CLXV. An economical person is the richest of all men, a miser is the poorest.

CLXVI. Sometimes apparent resemblances of character will bring two men together and for a certain time unite them. But their mistake gradually becomes evident, and they are astonished to find themselves not only far apart, but even repelled, in some sort, at all their points of contact.

CLXVII. Is it not curious to reflect that the glory of many a great man is to have spent his whole life in combating such prejudices or pitiable absurdities as ought never, on the face of them, to have entered any human mind. Bayle's greatness, for instance, lies in his having pointed out certain absurdities in philosophical and scholastic hair-splitting, over which a Gâtinais peasant of good natural intelligence would have shrugged his shoulders. That of Locke consists in having proved that we should never speak without understanding what we say, nor imagine we understand when we do not. That of other philosophers lies in having written enormous books directed against superstitions which a Canadian savage would contemptuously eschew. That of Montesquieu, and of certain authors before him, to have let it be dimly perceived, while still sparing a host of worthless prejudices, that governments are made for the governed and not the governed for the government. If ever that dream of the philosophers, a perfect Society, comes into being, what will posterity say when it sees the efforts that were necessary to achieve results so natural and so simple?

CLXVIII. A man owes it to himself, if he be both wise and honest, to join to that purity which satisfies his conscience a prudence capable of scenting out and forestalling calumny.

CLXIX. The lot of a far-seeing man is rather sad. He makes his friends uncomfortable by pointing out the misfortunes to which their imprudence exposes them. They do not believe him, and, when disaster comes, they take his prediction of it in ill part. Their pride makes them cast down their eyes in the company of this friend, who should have been their consolation, and whom they themselves would have sought out as such if they had not felt humiliated by his presence.

CLXX. The man who makes his happiness too subject to his reason, who submits it to examination, who, as it were, quibbles with his enjoyment and recognises only fastidious pleasures, will finish by having none at all. He is as one who makes his mattress smaller and smaller with assiduous carding until he ends by sleeping on the wood.

CLXXI. To borrow a phrase from the metaphysicians, time lessens the intensity of our *absolute* pleasures, but seems to heighten the force of our *relative* ones. I suspect that this is a trick of Nature to bind men to existence after the pleasant things which make life really delightful have passed away.

CLXXII. When we have been greatly tormented and wearied by our own sensibility, we realise that we ought to live from day to day, to forget much, and to *sponge out life* as fast as it passes.

CLXXIII. False modesty is the most becoming of all lies.

CLXXIV. They say that we should every day curtail our wants. This advice is supremely applicable to the wants of our pride: they are the most tyrannical and the most in need of suppression.

CLXXV. It is not unusual to see men of deficient spirit attempting to rise above their proper character by keeping company with lives of more vigorous temper. This gives birth to incongruities as pleasing as the pretension of a fool to wit.

CLXXVI. Virtue is no more the sovereign good than health is. It is rather the home appointed for that good than the good itself. It is more certain that vice makes man miserable than that virtue makes him happy. Its situation at the opposite pole from vice is the reason of virtue being so desirable.

CHAPTER III.

OF SOCIETY
OF GREAT PERSONAGES
OF RICHES
OF THE GENERAL PUBLIC

CLXXVII. It has been said that an understanding of the world can never be gained from books, but no one has previously given the reason for this; now you shall have it. Such understanding is the fruit of a thousand minute observations which pride would prevent us from confiding to any other, even our greatest friend. We are afraid of displaying a concern with trifles, even though trifles may be vital to the success of vast undertakings.

CLXXVIII. As we glance through the Memoirs and Records of the age of Louis the Fourteenth, we find something in the bad company of that time which is lacking in the good company of this.

CLXXIX. What is Society when reason does not form her ties, when feeling, within her, does not cast out interest, when an exchange of pleasant thoughts and true benevolence does not denote her? A fair, a brothel, an inn, a forest, some little houses on an evil site: she is all these in turn, and these things only, to the majority of those who are her members.

CLXXX. The metaphysical structure of Society may well be considered as a material edifice, built up of independent niches or compartments of varying size. These compartments and niches are the public Offices, with all the prerogatives and powers pertaining to them; and they continue though the people pass away. Sometimes they are filled by big men, sometimes by small; and not one, or hardly any one, is the right size for his position. Here you may see a giant stooping within his niche, and there a dwarf beneath a high arcade, for the space is rarely fashioned for the stature. A host of men of every size moves round the building, eager to seize whatever niche falls vacant. Each urges his birth or patron's favour as a claim for admission; but any man who put forward his suitability in size, the fit of sheath and weapon, would be laughed to scorn. Even his rivals forbear to object to their opponent's disproportion to the place at issue.

CLXXXI. We cannot live in Society when the time of our passions is passed. It is only tolerable during that age when we use our stomach for amusement and our person for killing time.

CLXXXII. Magistrates and men of the law know the court and all the interests of the day rather as students, who have been given an *exeat* and dined outside their college, may be said to know the world.

CLXXXIII. All that is said at receptions, or in *salons*, or during suppers, or at public gatherings, or even in books whose avowed object is an exposition of Society, is either false or quite inadequate. We may quote the Italian *per la predica*,[3] or the Latin *ad populum phaleras*[4] in this connection. We are more

[3] "for the sermon"

[4] "Display your trappings to the mob," a line from the *Satires* of Persius.

likely to hear useful truth when a reasonable citizen, who has seen much and seen it intelligently, speaks to a friend from his heart in the chimney corner. I have learnt more from such conversations than from all my reading or normal social intercourse; I have been set more surely on my way, and made to think more deeply.

CLXXXIV. We often have occasion to feel the power exerted over our emotions by the contrast of an idea with a physical or material object, and above all when the mind's transition from one to the other is abrupt and unexpected. You take a walk on the boulevard at evening, and pass a delightful garden fronting a tastefully illuminated *salon.* You catch a faint glimpse of beautiful women, of groves, of an alley, among the rest, winding away from you, filled with laughter. And there, from their slender forms, must be the nymphs. "Who is that one?" you ask, and someone answers: "It is Madame de B …, the mistress of the house." Unfortunately you happen to know her, and the spell is broken.

CLXXXV. When you meet the Baron de Breteuil, he chats about his successes, his uncouth love affairs, and ends by showing you a portrait of the Queen in a diamond rose.

CLXXXVI. A fool in his pride at some ribbon seems to me lower than that ridiculous fellow, who, during his pleasures, would have his mistress deck him behind with peacock feathers. He at least had the satisfaction of … But the other … ! The Baron de Breteuil is much lower than Peixoto.

CLXXXVII. De Breteuil's example shows us that we can carry about diamond-incrusted portraits of twelve or fifteen monarchs, and still be a fool.

CLXXXVIII. He is a fool; he is, in fact, a fool, and that is quickly said; but see how extreme you are in everything! For his foolishness amounts to—what? He mistakes his position for personality, his importance for merit, and his credit in the world for virtue. Is not everybody like this? Is there so much to make a fuss about?

CLXXXIX. When fools leave office, whether they have been ministers or senior clerks, an air of haughtiness or ridiculous importance hangs about them …

CXC. Acute observers have a thousand good tales to tell of the social folly and servility which they have witnessed; and we can see the same for ourselves in a hundred ready examples. The best proof of these evils being incurable is that they are as old as Monarchy itself. Indeed, countless anecdotes which I have heard have convinced me that, if monkeys had the parrot's gift, we would readily make them ministers.

CXCI. Nothing is so difficult to destroy as some trivial idea or accredited proverb. Louis the Fifteenth became bankrupt on three or four separate occasions, and yet we still swear on the *word of a gentleman.* M. de Guéménée's will carry no more weight.

CXCI I. People are no sooner herded into a mass than they think themselves in Society.

CXCIII. I have seen men outrage their consciences to please the wearer of a president's coif or judge's ermine. After this we cannot be surprised at those others who, for the coif itself or even the ermine, will sell their consciences outright. Both classes are vile, but the former are the more absurd.

CXCIV. Society is made up of two large divisions: those who have more dinners than appetite, and those who have more appetite than dinners.

CXCV. We give a meal costing ten or twenty louis to people with whom we have so little concern that we would not waste a shilling to buy a good digestion of our meal for one of them.

CXCVI. An excellent rule to observe in the art of jesting and mockery is this: the jester or mocker should be responsible for the success of his pleasantry with its victim, and should own himself in the wrong if the latter becomes annoyed.

CXCVII. M ... used to say that I laboured under one great misfortune: I could not get used to the omnipotence of fools. He was right. And I have noticed that a fool has this considerable advantage when he enters society: he finds himself among his equals. He is like Brother Lourdis in the Temple of Folly:

> *Everything pleased him, and at first he could*
> *Not realise he had left the Brotherhood.*

CXCVIII. Seeing the rogueries of little men and the extortions of the great in office, one is tempted to look upon Society as a wood infested by robbers, the most dangerous being the constables sent to arrest the others.

CXCIX. Both the Court and the general public give a conventional value to men and things, and then are surprised to find themselves deceived by it. This is as if arithmeticians should give a variable and arbitrary value to the figures in a sum, and then, after restoring their true and regular value in the addition, be astonished at the incorrectness of their answer.

CC. There are moments when Society seems really to value itself at its proper worth. I have frequently come to the conclusion that it looks up to those who care nothing at all about it. And, provided that this supreme contempt for the world be real, sincere and ingenuous, free from affectation and without boasting, it is often a man's best recommendation in the eyes of the world itself.

CCI. Society is so contemptible that the few honest men who abide there respect those who despise it, merely because they despise it.

CCII. Court friendship, fox faith and wolves' society.

CCIII. I would advise anyone who wishes a favour from a minister to approach him with a downcast air, rather than smiling. We do not love to see people happier than ourselves.

CCIV. It is a hard yet unavoidable truth that all things, even a seeming simplicity or open-handed kindness, are, in Society and above all in select society, matters of art, of science, and of calculation. I have met men in whom what appeared the grace of an unstudied movement was in reality an elaborate combination, swiftly conceived indeed, but as artificial as it was masterly. And I have seen very deliberate calculation wedded to the frankness of a most careless-seeming unreserve. It is the skilful disorder of a coquette's dress, where art has banished every hint of Art. And this artificiality, though disagreeable, is most necessary; for sorrow awaits that man who discovers his point of defect or vulnerable part, even to his closest companion. I have seen the intimate familiars of a man wounding his pride because they have pierced his secret; and it seems impossible in the present state of Society (by which I still mean the best society) that a man exists who could afford to show the deeps of his heart, the detail of his character, and above all his weakness, to his greatest friend. I repeat again that this refinement of behaviour is essential in that kind of society, and that a man has to carry it to a point beyond suspicion, if only not to be despised as the one bad actor in a troupe of excellent comedians.

CCV. People who think they love a Prince when they have just been treated well by him, remind me of children who want to be priests the day after a beautiful procession, or to be soldiers the day after they have witnessed a review.

CCVI. Favourites and persons in office occasionally take pains to attach to themselves men of undoubted merit, but from these they demand a preliminary degradation, and thus repel all those who have a sense of shame. I have met men, whom a favourite or minister ought to have been able to buy cheaply enough, quite as indignant at this condition as the most virtuous could be. One of such men once said to me: "The folk in power would like to buy our disgrace with promises rather than payment." They expect to purchase you, in fact, not with a lottery prize, but a lottery ticket; and I know some thorough-paced rogues who seem to be well treated by their patrons and are yet no nearer personal advantage than the most disinterested.

CCVII. Our useful, even brilliantly useful, actions and the most genuinely distinguished services we can render the Nation and even the Court itself, are, if we have not the Court's favour, nothing but splendid sins, as theologians say.

CCVIII. You cannot imagine how much intelligence it needs never to be ridiculous.

CCIX. Every man who lives much in society. convinces me of his lack of sensibility, for I can see scarcely anything in those surroundings calculated to engage the heart or do aught but harden it … except perhaps the sight of insensibility, frivolity and vanity sitting enthroned there.

CCX. When Princes break their miserable etiquette, it is always in favour of some girl or jester, and never for a man of worth. When women make themselves conspicuous, it is never for an upright man, always for a *creature.* In a word, when we throw off the yoke of public opinion, it is seldom for the purpose of rising above it, but nearly always to fall below.

CCXI. Some mistakes of behaviour are scarcely ever made in these days, or at least are made much more rarely. We have reached so great a pitch of refinement that even a quite unscrupulous man is taught, by the little thinking he has done, to abstain from certain platitudes which would have succeeded in former times; since thinking now can take the place of conscience. I have seen uncouth persons behave becomingly, with dignity, and without servility, before a prince or minister: a circumstance which misleads young people and novices, who do not know, or rather have forgotten, that a man ought to be judged by the *sum* of his character and principles.

CCXII. When we see the care which civil assemblies seem to have taken to banish merit from all Offices where it might be useful to Society, when we examine the league of fools against intelligence, we might suppose ourselves to be watching a conspiracy of valets to cast out their masters.

CCXIII. What does a young man find when he enters society? He finds people willing to protect him, professing to do him honour, and eager to lead and advise him. (For I say nothing of those who would willingly thrust him aside, or injure and cheat him.) If, therefore, he is of high enough spirit to desire no other protection than his own good conduct, or wish for honour from any person or circumstance outside himself, if his principles are his only guides, if his brains, his character, and his position (which last he can naturally determine better than any other) are his only counsellors, he will certainly be called eccentric, peculiar, and unmanageable. But if, on the other hand, he has little intelligence, few principles, and small nobility, if he does not know he is being ruled and patronised, if he becomes the ready instrument of those who have taken hold of him, he will be found quite charming, and, as the saying goes, "the best of fellows."

CCXIV. Society, what is called good society, is nothing but a struggle between a thousand opposing petty interests, an eternal warfare of all the vanities, each thwarting the other and clashing against the other, each wounded and humbled in turn, each paying with tomorrow's mortification of defeat for this day's victory. And yet they say that to live alone, and never be ruffled in that wretched conflict, where man draws every eye at one moment and then is overwhelmed the next, is not to live at all, is to be nothing. Wretched humanity!

CCXV. There is a certain profound insensibility to virtue which is more astonishing and shocking than vice itself. Most officials and those whom the vulgar public call great lords, or noble men, seem specially gifted with this odious quality. Is this, perhaps, the result of a vague, imperfectly developed idea on their part that men with virtue do not make suitable tools for intrigue? They certainly slight such men, as useless both to themselves and others in a land where success without intrigue, craft, and strategy is deemed impossible!

CCXVI. What do we see in Society? Everywhere either a simple and sincere respect for certain absurd conventions, for some stupidity (fools bow before their queen), or else a feigned regard for the same thing (since wise men fear their tyrant).

CCXVII. Driven by an absurd pride, the bourgeois make dung of their daughters for the fields of men of quality.

CCXVIII. Take twenty men, even honest ones, who are all acquainted with and all esteem some person of recognised merit, for instance, Dorilas; then speak favourably of him in their presence, and cry up his virtues and talents till all agree with you. "But what a pity he has not a larger fortune," says someone. "What do you mean," answers another. "He only lives without display because of his modesty. Do you know that he has an income of twenty-five thousand francs?" "Really?" "Really, and I can prove it…." Now let this worthy man make his appearance and compare his present welcome with the honourable but somewhat cold reception accorded him in the past…. He did so, he made his comparison, and groaned aloud; but there was one man whose greeting remained the same. "One out of twenty," said our philosopher, "I am content."

CCXIX. The life of the majority at Court! They let themselves be wearied and worn out, debased, enslaved and tormented for the most wretched ends. Before they can live, before they can be happy, they have to await the death of their enemies, of their rivals, and even of those they call their friends; and, while they are praying for these deaths, they dry up and wither and die themselves, asking news with their latest breath of the health of Monsieur So-and-So, of Madame So-and-So, who *will* not die.

CCXX. In spite of the foolish things which some contemporary physiognomists have written, it is quite certain that the habit of our thought can influence our expression in some of its aspects. Many courtiers have a deceitful eye for the same reason that most tailors are knock-kneed.

CCXXI. It is perhaps not true, though I have often heard it advanced, even by those who are themselves intelligent, that great fortunes imply the possession of intelligence on the part of those who gain them. It is much truer to say that there are certain proportions of intelligence and ability from which fortune finds it impossible to escape, even in men of absolute honesty … which, as we know, is fortune's greatest stumbling-block.

CCXXII. Montaigne's remark about greatness: "Let us slander it if we cannot attain it," though amusing and frequently true, is somewhat scandalous and puts a weapon into the hands of any fool whom fortune has favoured. Though it is often only our littleness which makes us hate all inequalities of station, it is quite possible for a truly wise and upright man to abhor these inequalities as barriers, keeping those hearts at a distance which nature purposed to be brought together. There are few men of exceptional character who have not, at one time or another, resisted their feelings for someone of higher rank and tortured themselves by repulsing a friendship which might have brought them comfort and delight. Instead of quoting Montaigne, these may say: "I abominate greatness, for it has kept me from one I loved, or might have loved."

CCXXIII. Whose associations are all quite honourable? Is there any man who does not keep company with someone for whom he has to apologise to his friends? Is there any woman who does not feel bound to explain to Society the visit of some other woman, whose presence at her house has caused surprise?

CCXXIV. If you are friends with a man at Court, a man of quality as the saying goes, and wish to inspire in him the most tender affection of which the human heart is capable, do not confine yourself to lavishing the cares of fondest friendship upon him, to easing his griefs, to comforting his afflictions, to giving him all your days, or to saving his life and honour as occasion serves. Do not, in fact, waste your time on trifles; do something further and finer, write his pedigree.

CCXXV. You believe that a minister in office holds such or such an opinion, because you have heard him say so; therefore you forebear to ask him for such or such a thing, the granting of which would contradict his favourite maxim. Later you will find that you have been imposed upon, and see the man do things which prove that a minister has no principles at all, but only the knack or bad habit of saying … such and such.

CCXXVI. Many courtiers get themselves hated without profit, merely for the pleasure of being so. They are like lizards whose crawling has gained them nought but the loss of their tails.

CCXXVII. This man is forever unworthy of consideration: he should make his fortune and live with the riffraff.

CCXXVIII. Bodies of men—Parliaments, Academies, Convocations—may disgrace themselves as they will; they are upheld by their mass, and we can do nothing against them.

Dishonour and ridicule glance off them, as gun shot off a boar or crocodile.

CCXXIX. Seeing what passes in Society, the greatest misanthrope would at last grow merry, and Heraclitus die of laughing.

CCXXX. Given an equality of brains and judgment, it seems to me that a man who is born rich can never know Nature, Society and the human heart as well as a poor man. For, during that moment of time which the first fills with a pleasure, the second is comforting himself with a reflection....

CCXXXI. When we see Princes acting creditably on their own initiative, we are apt to blame those about them for the greater number of their misdeeds and weaknesses. "How unlucky," we say, "that this Prince should have such friends as Damis and Aramont!" We do not reflect that, if Damis and Aramont had been men of any nobility or resolution, they would not have had such a friend as the Prince.

CCXXXII. In proportion as Philosophy advances, folly redoubles its efforts to establish the reign of prejudice. Consider the vogue given by the present government to ideas of gentility. This has reached such a point that there are no longer more than two estates of women: ladies of quality and mistresses: the rest are of no account. It is not virtue, but only vice, that can raise a woman above her station now.

CCXXXIII. To gain fortune and esteem without the advantage of having ancestors, and over the heads of so many people who have done all that is needful sheerly by being born, is to win or draw a game of chess in which we are giving a castle. When our rivals have other conventional advantages also, we must abandon the game. We can give a castle, but not the queen.

CCXXXIV. Those who bring up Princes and profess to give them a good education, after they themselves have submitted to the forms and degrading ceremonies which surround their charges, are like teachers of arithmetic who din into their pupils that three and three make eight, and then hope to mould them into mathematicians.

CCXXXV. What man is the most a stranger to those about him? A Frenchman in Peking or Macao? A Laplander in Senegal? Or might it not be, I wonder, a deserving person without gold or pedigree in the midst of men who have got one or both? Is it not strange that Society should still endure, with its tacit agreement to exclude nineteen-twentieths of Society from sharing its privileges?

CCXXXVI. Society and the World are like a library where at first glance all seems in order, for the books are arranged according to their shapes and sizes, but where, on closer scrutiny, there is seen to be utter confusion, because there has been no grouping under subject matter, class, or author.

CCXXXVII. To have great and even illustrious friendships is no longer to be counted a merit in a land where a man frequently becomes popular by his vices and is sought after because of his follies.

CCXXXVIII. There are some men who, while not being in the least agreeable themselves, do not prevent this quality in others. Therefore their company is sometimes tolerable. But there is a different kind of disagreeable person, whose very presence can blast the unfolding of amiability in his fellows. Such men are insupportable: and this is the great disadvantage of pedantry.

CCXXXIX. Experience, which enlightens the private citizen, corrupts all Ministers and Princes.

CCXL. The modern public is like modern Tragedy, ridiculous, cruel, insipid.

CCXLI. People have tried to turn the trade of *Courtier* into a science. Everyone seeks to rise.

CCXLII. Most of the relationships in public life, such as coalition and the rest, stand in the same relation to friendship as cicisbeism does to love.

CCXLIII. The art of parenthesis is one of the great secrets of social eloquence.

CCXLIV. Be he Prince of the blood, hebdomadary chaplain, quarter surgeon, or apothecary, everyone at Court is a courtier.

CCXLV. Magistrates charged with maintaining public order, such as the criminal, civil, and police commissioners, and many another, nearly always end up with a terrible opinion of Society. They think they know mankind, when they only know the refuse of mankind; a town is not judged by its sewers or a house by its latrines. Most magistrates remind one of school castigators who have a small den near the privies, and only leave it to employ their whips.

CCXLVI. Mockery should do justice on all the faults of man and of Society. By the help of mockery we avoid exposing ourselves; and we put everything in its proper place by mockery, without descending from our own. Mockery proves that we are greater than the qualities and men we ridicule, and yet our victims cannot take offence unless they would seem deficient in humour or manners. A reputation for skill with this weapon gives a man of inferior rank the same sort of reputation in the society of his betters as soldiers accord to an exceptional swordsman. I have heard a wit remark that, if they dethroned mockery, he would leave Society tomorrow. Mockery is a kind of bloodless duel which, like the other sort, makes men more circumspect and more polite.

CCXLVII. At first sight we do not suspect the evil wrought by an ambition to earn that most familiar eulogy that "Monsieur So-and-So is very kind." It happens, I know not how, that there is a sort of easiness, carelessness, helplessness, and unreason which, when tempered with a certain wit, are found most pleasing. It also happens that a man with whom we can do what we like, a man who belongs to the moment, is better company than one of method, resolution, and principle, who does not forget his friend when his friend is ill or absent, who will leave a party of pleasure to do him service. It would be tedious to compile a list of those shortcomings, errors, and bad habits which can give social pleasure. Suffice it that men of the world, who have studied the art of pleasing more deeply than we or even they suppose, have a majority of all those faults: this comes from their necessity of hearing said that "Monsieur So-and-So is very kind."

CCXLVIII. There are some things not to be guessed at by a well-born youth. If one were twenty how could one mistrust a police spy with the *cordon rouge?*

CCXLIX. The most absurd customs and the most ridiculous ceremonies live, in France and elsewhere, under the shadow of the phrase: *it is the fashion.* And Hottentots counter with exactly the same reason when Europeans ask them why they eat grasshoppers or devour their body lice. *It is the fashion*, they explain.

CCL. The most unjust and preposterous claim, one which would be ridiculed in any gathering of reputable men, may become the subject of a lawsuit, and thenceforward be declared legitimate;

for any case may be lost or won in the courts, just as the most crazy and ludicrous opinion may be accepted wherever men meet in a body, and the wisest dismissed with contempt. It is only a question of presenting either opinion as a party matter; and nothing is easier to do than this, since nearly all of man's congregations are divided by party.

CCLI. What would a fop be without his foppery? A butterfly without its wings would be a caterpillar.

CCLII. Courtiers are poor men who have become rich by begging.

CCLIII. It is easy enough to reduce the exact value of celebrity to simple terms: the man who becomes known for a particular talent or virtue lays himself open to the passive good will of a few upright persons, and the active malevolence of all baser men. Count the two classes, and weigh the two forces.

CCLIV. Few people can love a philosopher. He who, in the midst of man's pretension and the shams of circumstance, says to each man and thing: *I take you for what you are; I assess you at what you are worth*, is almost a public enemy. And it is no slight undertaking to win love and esteem in the face of this declared and steadfast purpose.

CCLV. When the evils of Society in general, and the horrors presented to our sight by the Capital or the larger towns, shock us too greatly, we should say: "Still worse misfortunes might have sprung from the combination which has set twenty-five million souls beneath the rule of one, and herded seven hundred thousand men into a space of two square leagues."

CCLVI. Superlative qualities often unfit a man for Society. We do not take ingots with us when we go to market, but silver or small change.

CCLVII. That thing which people call the world, society with its *Salons* and Circles, is a bad play, or if you will a worthless opera, quite uninteresting, but helped out a little by its stage mechanism and decoration.

CCLVIII. To have an accurate idea of things, we must understand words in an opposite sense to that which Society gives them. For example, Misanthropist means Philanthropist; a bad Frenchman means a good citizen who has been drawing attention to monstrous abuses; and a Philosopher is a simple-minded man who knows that two and two make four.

CCLIX. Nowadays an artist paints your portrait in seven minutes, another imparts his art to you in three days, and a third man teaches you English in forty lessons. They are ready to instruct you in eight languages by the use of pictures which show you various things, with their names in those eight languages underneath them. I suppose if they could compress all the pleasures, sensations, and ideas of a lifetime into a single twenty-four hours, they would do so, and make you swallow the pill, and say: "Be off!"

CCLX. We must not regard Burrhus as an absolutely virtuous person; he only has this quality when compared with Narcissus. Seneca and Burrhus are the honest men of an age which had no honest men.

CCLXI. If we would please in society, we must be prepared to learn many things we know from men who do not know them.

CCLXII. Men whom we only half know, and things which we know three-quarters only, we do not know at all. These two reflections are sufficient to make us excellent judges of nearly all the conversations in the world.

CCLXIII. In a land where everyone strives to *seem*, many people may be expected to believe, and do in fact believe, that it is better to be a bankrupt than to be nothing.

CCLXIV. The danger of a *neglected cold* is to doctors what Purgatory is to priests, an *Eldorado.*

CCLXV. Conversations are like voyages: we hardly feel it when we put to sea, and do not notice that we have left the shore until we are far away from it.

CCLXVI. A thoughtful man maintains, in the presence of certain millionaires, that it is quite possible to be happy on an income of two thousand crowns. This they deny with acrimony and even anger; so that, on leaving their presence, he casts about for the reason of such bitterness on the part of people who are really his friends. At last he finds that it is this: his argument made them realise that he was not dependent on them. Any man with few needs appears a menace to the rich for he is always in a position to escape from them, and the tyrants see that thus they lose a slave. The same principle has a general application to the other passions. The indifference of a man who has conquered his tendency to fall in love is always detestable to women. At once they cease to take any interest in him; and this is perhaps the reason why no one concerns himself with the fortunes of a Philosopher: his passions are not those which touch Society. It is clear that hardly anything can be done to give him happiness; and with that we leave him.

CCLXVII. It is dangerous for a Philosopher attached to the train of a great man (if ever, that is, great men have kept Philosophers) to proclaim his full disinterestedness, for he may be taken at his word. Rather he finds it necessary to conceal his true feelings and to become, as it were, hypocritically ambitious.

CHAPTER IV.

OF THE TASTE FOR RETIREMENT, AND DIGNITY OF CHARACTER

CCLXVIII. A philosopher looks upon what they call *a position in the world* much as the Tartars look upon towns, that is to say, as a prison. For it is a circle where ideas contract and work in upon themselves, denying all breadth or development to the mind and soul. The man who has a great position in the world possesses a more ornate and larger prison; the man with a small position lies in a dungeon. He who has no position at all is the sole free citizen; and even he is not entirely free, unless he lives in comfortable circumstances, or at least has no need of his fellows.

CCLXIX. If he is forced to live in this world in a state of poverty, the most modest man should adopt an assured carriage and a certain ease of manner, to prevent others from taking advantage of him. In fact he should, in these circumstances, deck out his modesty in pride.

CCLXX. It is weakness of character, or lack of ideas, it is all, in a word, that can prevent them from living with themselves, which saves so many people from misanthropy.

CCLXXI. Is not the reason for our being happier in solitude than in Society the fact that in solitude we think of things, and in Society are forced to think of men.

CCLXXII. The thoughts of a recluse, provided he have any understanding at all, and however ordinary he may be in other ways, would have little value if they were not worth at least as much as the things which are said and done in Society.

CCLXXIII. A man who obstinately refuses to allow his reason, his probity, or at least his feelings of delicacy to bend beneath the weight of any of the absurd or dishonest conventions of Society, a man who never bows when it is to his interest to bow, will infallibly end without support of any kind, and with one friend only: an abstract being called virtue, who leaves him to die of hunger.

CCLXXIV. We must not refuse to live with all save those who can appreciate us: that would be the demand of too delicate a vanity, and one too difficult to satisfy; but, at the same time, we ought only to lay the foundation of our daily life among men who are capable of a sense of our value. Even a Philosopher would not blame this kind of self-esteem.

CCLXXV. People sometimes say of a man who lives alone: *He does not like Society;* but this is very often the same as saying that a man does not like walking because he will not willingly walk at evening in the forest of Bondy.

CCLXXVI. Is it quite certain that a man whose reason is perfectly honest and whose moral sense is perfectly balanced can live with any other person? By living I do not mean being together without coming to blows, I mean enjoying existence together, loving each other, and taking delight in each other's company.

CCLXXVII. An intelligent man is lost if he does not add strength of character to his intelligence. When one has the lantern of Diogenes, one should carry his stick also.

CCLXXVIII. No one in the world has more enemies than a self-respecting and intelligent person who would rather leave men and things for what they are, than take them for what they are not.

CCLXXIX. Society hardens the heart of most persons; and those who are least susceptible to this process are obliged to create a sort of factitious insensibility, to escape being practised upon by either men or women. The feeling of an upright character, after having been delivered over to Society for a few days, is ordinarily one of painful depression; but this sentiment has a single advantage, it makes seclusion delightful.

CCLXXX. The thoughts of the public can hardly ever be other than mean and sordid, for it hears of scarcely anything save scandal and conspicuous indecency, and naturally paints the greater part of all facts and conversations which reach it in the selfsame colours. Though these intimacies be of the most honourable kind, if it notices a great noble on friendly terms with a man of merit, or an office holder with a private person, it sees no more in the first case than a patron and his client, and, in the second, than intrigue or espionage. To it a generous action, where every incident is lofty and affecting, means only that money has been lent to a clever trickster by his dupe. And when it hears gossip of what is frequently a noble and touching passion between admirable man and woman, it pictures either harlotry or license. The judgments of the public are predetermined by the great number of cases where it has been forced into condemnation and contempt; and it follows that the best thing which can happen to an honourable man is to escape the public altogether.

CCLXXXI. Nature never said to me: *Do not be poor;* still less did she say: *Be rich;* her cry to me was always: *Be independent.*

CCLXXXII. As the Philosopher prides himself on giving no more than their true value to all men, it is not surprising that his verdicts are universally considered unpleasant.

CCLXXXIII. The man of the world, the friend of fortune, and even the lover of glory, draws a straight line before him which leads to an unknown end. But the man who is his own companion, the wise man, describes a circle whose finish is with himself. He is the *totus teres atque rotundus*[5] of Horace.

CCLXXXIV. We need not be surprised at Jean-Jacques Rousseau's taste for solitude; such souls are condemned, like the eagle, to loneliness and

[5] "whole, smooth and rounded"

isolation; but they are also like the eagle in this, that the loftiness of their flight and the great compass of their vision make up the charm of their retirement.

CCLXXXV. He who has no character is not a man, but a thing.

CCLXXXVI. People have found the *moi* of Medea sublime, but the man who cannot say the same in all the accidents of life, is little or nothing.

CCLXXXVII. Unless we know a man very well, we do not know him at all; and few are worth the studying. From this it follows that a person of genuine worth should not, as a rule, be anxious for others to have knowledge of him. He is well aware that few can appreciate his excellence and that each in this small company has ties and interest and pride of place which prevent him from giving that excellence its due regard. And it would, of course, be impossible for true merit to be flattered by the threadbare panegyrics which the vulgar accord to it, when they chance to suspect its existence.

CCLXXXVIII. When a man's character has raised his reputation to such a pitch that his conduct, on all occasions when probity is at stake, may be anticipated, both rogues and the half-honest cry him down and carefully avoid him. And, more than this, entirely honest men, convinced by his principles that they will find him at their side in every encounter where they have need of him, now pass him by and hasten to make sure of others, of whom they are doubtful.

CCLXXXIX. Nearly all men are slaves, for that reason which the Spartans gave for the slavery of the Persians, because they cannot pronounce the single syllable *no.* To be able to say this word and to be able to live alone are the two sole means of retaining liberty and character.

CCXC. When we have resolved only to frequent the society of those who can treat with us on terms of morality and virtue, reason and truth, who can look upon conventions, vanities, and ceremonials simply as the props of civil Society … when we have taken this resolve, I say, (and, unless we would admit to foolishness, weakness, or villainy, we ought certainly to take it) the result will be a life of almost complete seclusion.

CCXCI. Every man who knows himself to entertain noble sentiments has the right to go outside his character—rather than to recede from his position —if by so doing he can make men treat him as he deserves.

CHAPTER V.

MORAL CONSIDERATIONS

CCXCII. Philosophers recognise these four principle virtues, from which they derive all others: justice, temperance, courage, and prudence. The last may be said to comprehend the two first, justice and temperance, and to do duty, in some sort, for the third, by sparing the man who has the misfortune to be deficient in courage many of the occasions on which this quality is needed.

CCXCIII. Moralists and Philosophers, in building up Physical and Metaphysical systems, have multiplied their maxims excessively and made them too general. What becomes, for example, of the saying of Tacitus: *Neque femina, amissa pudicitia, alia abnuerit*,[6] when we consider the example of those many women in whom a single frailty has not prevented the practice of several virtues? I myself have observed Mme. de L…, whose youth differed but little from that of Manon Lescaut, conceive a passion in her maturity, worthy of Heloïse. But these examples hold a conclusion dangerous to adduce in print, and it is only to prevent ourselves being gulled by the quackery of Moralists that we need to note them.

CCXCIV. Society has banished from evil living all that might shock good taste. This reformation is only ten years old.

---

[6] "When a woman has lost her chastity, she will refuse nothing"

CCXCV. When the soul is sick she acts in exactly the same fashion as the body, restlessly tossing until at last she finds a certain peace. In the end she settles on that system of feelings and ideas most necessary to her repose.

CCXCVI. There are some people to whom illusions are as necessary, in all that concerns them, as their life itself. If sometimes they show glimmerings of observation which make us think they are nearing the truth, they straightway sheer off again, like children who run after a masquerade and then take flight as soon as it turns back.

CCXCVII. Our gratitude to most benefactors is the same as our feeling for dentists who have pulled our teeth. We acknowledge the good they have done and the evil from which they have delivered us, but we remember the pain they have occasioned and do not love them very much.

CCXCVIII. A fastidious benefactor should reflect that there is a material side to his service, of which the beneficiary should be spared all thought. The idea of it must, as it were, be wrapped and hidden away in the sentiment which has prompted the benefit, just as with lovers the thought of the physical act is draped and ennobled in the magic of the love which leads to it.

CCXCIX. Each benefit received is either near to the heart or else entirely odious; a reliquary or dead man's bone, fit to enshrine … or trample under foot.

CCC. Most professedly anonymous benefactors take flight, after their good deed, rather in the style of Virgil's Galatea: *Et se cupit ante videri.*[7]

CCCI. We are commonly supposed to bind folk to ourselves by being good to them. This is a kindness of Nature, for it is just that love should be the recompense of service …

CCCII. Scandal is an importunate wasp, against which we must make no movement unless we are quite sure that we can kill it; otherwise it will return to the attack more furious than ever.

CCCIII. The new friends we make after a certain age, in the hope of replacing old friends who are lost, are to those same old friends as glass eyes and false teeth and wooden legs to natural eyes and teeth, and legs of flesh and bone.

CCCIV. There is sometimes a very pleasant philosophy to be discovered in the innocencies of a well-born child.

CCCV. Most friendships so bristle with *ifs* and *buts*, that they come very near to mere acquaintanceship, dependent on *understandings.*

CCCVI. Our customs and the customs of antiquity have as much in common as Aristides, Superintendent General of Athens, and the Abbé Terray.

---

[7] "She departs, and desires to be seen going"

CCCVII. Evil by nature, mankind has become much more so through Society, whose every member contributes the defects, first of humanity, then of the individual, and lastly of the social order to which he belongs. These shortcomings grow more pronounced with time, so that a man, offended by them in others, as his age advances, and made unhappy by their presence in himself, conceives a contempt for both Mankind and Society, and has to direct it against one or other.

CCCVIII. It is with happiness as with watches. The least complicated watch goes the least wrong, and the repeater is the most subject to variation. Should it also mark the minutes the likelihood of its breaking down is greater, and a watch which sets out to indicate the day of the week and the month of the year is all the more liable to go wrong.

CCCIX. Man's joys and griefs are equally in vain, but a gold or azure soap-bubble is better than a black or grey one.

CCCX. A man who masks tyranny, patronage, or even charity behind the likeness and title of friendship, reminds me of that infamous priest who did his poisoning with holy wafers.

CCCXI. There are few benefactors who do not say with Satan: *Si cadens adoraveris me.*[8]

CCCXII. Poverty marks down the price of crime.

---

[8] "if you fall down and adore me"

CCCXIII. Stoics are a sort of inspired persons who carry poetic exaltation and enthusiasm into the sphere of morals.

CCCXIV. If it were possible for a man to lack intelligence himself and yet have the power to recognise grace, subtlety, comprehension, and every mental quality in another, and to show that he did so, his society, though unproductive, would be eagerly cultivated. Postulate the same of spiritual qualities and a like result obtains.

CCCXV. When we see or experience the pains inseparable from extreme feeling either in love or friendship, from the death of one we adore or from life's accidents, we are tempted to believe that dissipation and frivolity are not great follies after all, and that the world is worth little more than the use to which worldly people put it.

CCCXVI. In certain passionate friendships we have all of passion's delight and the approbation of reason into the bargain.

CCCXVII. Deep and delicate friendships have often been wounded by a crumpled rose.

CCCXVIII. Generosity is only the compassion of a lofty soul.

CCCXIX. To enjoy yourself and make others enjoy themselves, without harming yourself or any other; that, to my mind, is the whole of ethics.

CCCXX. As far as they regard genuinely honest people of fixed principles, the Commandments of God have been written in little on the face of the Abbey of Thélème: *Do what you will.*

CCCXXI. Education should rest on the dual support of moral philosophy and prudence, moral philosophy as the stay of virtue, and prudence as a shield against the vice in others. If you tip the scale on the moral side you will produce none but dupes and martyrs, and by tilting it in the other direction you will develop a quality of selfish calculation only. Justice to oneself and to others is the first principle of all Society; and if we should love our neighbour as ourself, it is quite as just that we should love ourself as much as our neighbour.

CCCXXII. Perfect friendship alone can develop the full qualities of soul and mind in certain people; ordinary intercourse unfolds a few pleasing qualities in them, that is all. They are fine fruit-trees which only reach maturity in the sunshine, and in a hothouse bring forth nothing but pleasant and useless foliage.

CCCXXIII. When I was young and subject to the urge of my passions, which enticed me into society and drove me to seek in pleasure and among my fellows some diversion from the cruel discomforts to which I was a prey, the delights of seclusion and hard work were preached at me, and I was wearied to death by pedantic sermons in their favour. But now that I am forty and have lost those passions which make society tolerable, now that I find nothing in it save meanness and futility, and have no further need of my kind as an escape from torment, the inclination for labour and retirement has grown strong in me, to the exclusion of all other feelings. For this reason I have withdrawn from society; and now I am incessantly pestered to go back to it! I am accused of misanthropy and other failings! What conclusion may we draw from this fantastic disparity? Man's need to censure everything.

CCCXXIV. I am a student only of what pleases me, and but exercise my brain on such ideas as it finds interesting. They may turn out to be useful either to myself or others, or they may turn out to be useless. Time may or may not bring circumstances in its train which will render my stores of knowledge profitable. In either case, I shall have enjoyed the inestimable advantage of having done nothing against the grain, of having lived up to my opinions and my character.

CCCXXV. I have destroyed my passions rather as a violent rider may kill his horse, because he cannot govern it.

CCCXXVI. The first occasions of my grief have served me as chain-mail against the others.

CCCXXVII. I still entertain for M. de la Borde that feeling which any well-bred man must have on passing a friend's tomb.

CCCXXVIII. I certainly have things to complain of, and perhaps men; but I keep silence about the men and only complain about the things. If I avoid the company of the former it is solely that I would not live with those who make me bear the burden of the latter.

CCCXXIX. In order to reach me, Fortune must comply with those conditions which my character imposes upon her.

CCCXXX. When my heart feels need of tenderness, I recall the loss of friends who are no longer with me and of women death has taken. I live in their graves, and send my spirit to wander about theirs. I have, alas, three tombs.

CCCXXXI. I feel punished and not rewarded, when I have done good and it chances to be discovered.

CCCXXXII. By giving up Society and Fortune I found happiness, peace and health, and even riches. Also I found, in spite of the proverb, that he who abandons the game shall win it.

CCCXXXIII. Celebrity is the reproof of merit, the punishment of genius. I consider mine, such as it is, as an informer, born to trouble my repose. As I destroy it, I feel the joy of triumphing over an enemy. Sensibility with me has even conquered self-esteem, and my vanity of authorship died in the destruction of my interest in men.

CCCXXXIV. True and tender friendship will suffer no alloy of other sentiment. I count it great happiness that friendship had already been perfectly established between M. de M …[9] and myself before I had the opportunity of rendering him that service which I did render, and of which I alone was capable. If a suspicion had been possible that all he had done for me was dictated by an expectation of finding me such as he did find me in that particular circumstance, if it had been possible for him to have foreseen the circumstance itself, my happiness would have been poisoned for all time.

CCCXXXV. My whole life is woven of threads which are in blatant contrast to my principles. I have no liking for Princes, and yet am attached to both a Prince and a Princess; I am famous for republican maxims, and yet many of my friends are covered with orders of monarchy; I love self-chosen poverty, and live among rich people; I avoid all honours, and yet some have come to me. Literature is almost my only consolation, and yet I meet no distinguished intellects and never go to the Academy. Moreover, I believe that illusions are necessary to man, yet live without illusion; I believe that the passions are more profitable than reason, and yet no longer know what passion is …

CCCXXXVI. I know nothing of what I have learned, I have divined the little I still know.

---

[9] Mirabeau

CCCXXXVII. One of the great misfortunes of

mankind is that even his good qualities are sometimes useless to him, and that the art of employing and well directing them is often the latest fruit of his experience.

CCCXXXVIII. Indecision and anxiety are to the mind and soul as is the Extraordinary Question to the body.

CCCXXXIX. An honest fellow stripped of all his illusions is the ideal man. Though he may have little wit, his society is always pleasant. As nothing matters to him, he cannot be pedantic; yet is he tolerant, remembering that he too has had the illusions which still beguile his neighbour. He is trustworthy in his dealings, because of his indifference; he avoids all quarrelling and scandal in his own person, and either forgets or passes over such gossip or bickering as may be directed against himself. He is more entertaining than other people because he is in a constant state of epigram against his neighbour. He dwells in truth, and smiles at the stumbling of others who grope in falsehood. He watches from a lighted place the ludicrous antics of those who walk in a dim room at random. Laughing, he breaks the false weight and measure of men and things.

CCCXL. We are startled at violent means, but they suit strong natures well enough; and vigorous spirits depend on the extreme …

CCCXLI. The contemplative life is often a wretched one. We ought to do more, and think less, and not watch ourselves living.

CCCXLII. Man may aspire to virtue, but he cannot reasonably aspire to truth.

CCCXLIII. The Jansenism of Christianity is simply pagan Stoicism degraded in form and brought within reach of the Christian rabble. And this sect has Pascals and Arnauds to defend it!

CHAPTER VI.

OF WOMEN
OF LOVE, MARRIAGE,
AND GALLANTRY

CCCXLIV. I am ashamed of your opinion of me; I have not always been as Céladon[10] as you see me now. If I told you three or four incidents of my youth you would see that it was not too impeccable, and had been passed in the best of company.

CCCXLV. If love is to appear disinterested it must be made of love alone, must solely live and feed on love.

CCCXLVI. When I see infatuation in a woman, or in a man for that matter, I begin to suspect a lack of sensibility. This rule has never failed me.

CCCXLVII. A sentiment that can be valued has no value.

CCCXLVIII. Love is like an epidemic: the more we fear it, the more we are prone to catch it.

CCCXLIX. A man in love always tries to be more agreeable than he is; that is why nearly all lovers are ridiculous.

CCCL. Some women have made themselves miserable for life, have ruined and dishonoured themselves, because a man has killed their love for him by managing his powder clumsily, or cutting

[10] A generic name in pastoral poetry for a rustic lover.

one of his nails unskilfully, or putting on a stocking inside out.

CCCLI. A proud disinterested spirit, having felt great passions, thenceforward fears and avoids them; especially he disdains all petty gallantry, as one who has known friendship disdains acquaintance and the little partnerships of every day.

CCCLII. It is often asked why women parade their men, and most of the answers given are derogatory to the latter. The real reason is that this is the only way in which women can savour their empire to the full.

CCCLIII. Middle-class women who entertain the hope or fancy of being something in the world, lose Nature's happiness and miss Society's. They are the most unfortunate creatures I have known.

CCCLIV. Society diminishes men, and reduces women to nothing.

CCCLV. Women frequently entertain fancies and infatuations, sometimes feel liking, and even, occasionally, ascend to the level of passion. Steadfast affection is the sentiment of which they are least capable. They are formed for converse with our weakness and folly, not with our reason. Physical and surface sympathies abound between their sex and ours, but intellectual, spiritual, and moral affinities are very rare. This is proved by the scant consideration they have for a man of forty, even when they are getting near that age themselves. If at any time they favour such a one, you will find that it is for some dishonourable end, or through calculated selfishness; and then the exception more than proves the rule. Nor in this instance is it fair to say: Who proves too much proves nothing.

CCCLVI. It is by self-love that love seduces us; for how can we resist a feeling which enhances what we have in our own sight, restores what we have lost, and gives us what we have not?

CCCLVII. When a man and a woman have an overwhelming passion for each other, it seems to me, in spite of such obstacles dividing them as parents or husband, that they belong to each other in the *name of Nature*, and are lovers by *Divine right*, in spite of human convention or the laws.

CCCLVIII. Take the self-love from love, and very little remains. Once love is purged of vanity it is like a feeble convalescent, scarce able to drag itself about.

CCCLIX. Love, as it is practised in Society, is but the exchange of two caprices and the contact of two skins.

CCCLX. When they wish to persuade me to visit such and such a woman, people sometimes say: "she is very lovable." As if I wanted to love her! They had much better have said: "she is very loving," for men are more eager to be loved than anxious to love.

CCCLXI. If you would estimate the extent of a woman's pride in youth, see how much remains even after she has passed the age of pleasing!

CCCLXII. Speaking of women's favours, M. de … used to say: It is an auction room business, and neither feeling nor merit are ever successful bidders.

CCCLXIII. Young women share this disadvantage with Kings, that they can have no friend. But happily, also, they seem to feel their loss as little. The greatness of Kings and the vanity of young women steal all their sensibility away.

CCCLXIV. In the political world they say that a wise man makes no conquests: this might pass for truth in the gallant world as well.

CCCLXV. It is a pleasant thought that the phrase *to know a woman*, even in many ancient languages and among the simple peoples who have lived nearest to Nature, means to go to bed with her; as if it were quite impossible to know a woman without doing so. If the patriarchs had made this discovery they were more advanced than is usually supposed.

CCCLXVI. In the war between men and women, the former have this great advantage: the unvirtuous among the enemy are on their side.

CCCLXVII. There are girls who can sell, but cannot give themselves.

CCCLXVIII. The noblest love unlocks the gate of the soul to little passions; and marriage unlocks the gate of the soul to the little passions of one's wife: ambition, vanity, and such.

CCCLXIX. However fine and well-disposed you are, and however unimaginably perfect the woman you love, you will never be quite able to forgive her your predecessor, or your successor.

CCCLXX. Perhaps one should have experienced love in order to know friendship.

CCCLXXI. Men's commerce with women is an armed commerce, such as Europeans carry on in India.

CCCLXXII. For a man's intimacy with a woman to be really interesting to him, there must be either gratification, memory, or desire between them.

CCCLXXIII. A witty woman once told me something which may well be the genuine secret of her sex: that in choosing a lover each one of her kind takes more account of how other women regard him than of how she regards him herself.

CCCLXXIV. To prove her great passion for him, although she has not got one, Mme. de … has gone to rejoin her lover in England. Nowadays even scandal is governed by public opinion.

CCCLXXV. I remember hearing a man forswear the Opera girls, because, as he said, he had found them as false as honest women.

CCCLXXVI. The ear and the mind go in for gossip, not so the heart.

CCCLXXVII. Feeling creates thought, men willingly agree; but they will not so willingly agree that thought creates feeling, though this is scarcely less true.

CCCLXXVIII. What is a mistress? A woman at whose side one forgets what one has learned by heart, the manifold blemishes of the sex.

CCCLXXIX. Time has replaced the sauce of mystery by the sauce of scandal in our love affairs.

CCCLXXX. It would seem that love never seeks real perfection, and even fears it. It delights only in the perfection it has itself imagined; it is like those kings who recognise no greatness except in their own works.

CCCLXXXI. Naturalists tell us that degeneration begins through the female in every animal species. Philosophers of social civilisation might affirm the same in ethics.

CCCLXXXII. The zest of intimacy with women lies in the multitude of *understandings* inseparable from it; for though *understandings* between men are vexatious, or at least insipid, they are pleasant enough between man and woman.

CCCLXXXIII. It is a common saying that the most beautiful woman in the world can only give what she has. This is entirely false. She gives exactly what the recipient thinks he has received; for imagination fixes the value in this sort of favour.

CCCLXXXIV. Indecency and lack of shame are absurd in all systems of philosophy: as much in those which insist upon abstinence as in those which encourage enjoyment.

CCCLXXXV. I have noticed in reading the Scriptures that when the author wishes to reproach Humanity for its passions or crimes, he speaks of the *children of men;* but substitutes *man born of woman* when he is dealing with folly or weakness.

CCCLXXXVI. Man would be too wretched in a woman's presence if he remembered the least item of certain matters which he has by heart.

CCCLXXXVII. In giving man an absolutely ineradicable taste for women, Nature seems to have foreseen that without it man's contempt for the vices of the sex, and principally for its vanity, would have gravely prejudiced the maintenance and propagation of the race.

CCCLXXXVIII. A man once told me quite seriously that one who had not visited plenty of *girls* could not know women; he was a great admirer of his own wife, who deceived him.

CCCLXXXIX. Marriage and Celibacy are both evils: it is better to choose the one which is not incurable.

CCCXC. In love it is sufficient for the good qualities and graces of each party to please the other; but in a happy marriage the very faults of husband and wife must be mutually delightful or at least agreeable.

CCCXCI. Love is a pleasanter thing than marriage, for the same reason that the Romans are more amusing than History.

CCCXCII. Hymen comes after Love, smoke after fire.

CCCXCIII. The wisest and most exact statement ever made about Celibacy and Marriage was that, whichever your choice, you would repent of it. Fontenelle in his old age was sorry that he had not married; but by that time a matter of ninety-five care-free years had slipped his memory.

CCCXCIV. The reasonable aspect of marriage is its only advantage, the foolish its only attraction; what lies between is but a base calculation.

CCCXCV. Woman must be married before she is or can be anything. Her husband is a kind of labourer who teases her body, rough-hews her intellect, and puts a half polish on her soul.

CCCXCVI. Marriage, as it obtains among the great, is a kind of conventional indecency.

CCCXCVII. We have heard men who pass for respectable, and whole collections of well-considered people, congratulate Mlle …, a young, beautiful, virtuous and entertaining lady, on her marriage with M. …, a diseased, repulsive, disingenuous, imbecile and rich old man. If one thing more than another characterises this lamentable century it is the possibility of such ridiculous congratulation, such reversal of every natural and moral instinct.

CCCXCVIII. Husbands labour under this disadvantage, that the wittiest can be everywhere superfluous, even in his own home; can be boring if he does not speak, and ridiculous if he says the simplest thing. His wife's love may relieve a part of this embarrassment; that is why M. … said to his lady: "My dear friend, help me not to be ridiculous."

CCCXCIX. Divorce is so entirely natural that, in many houses, he sleeps each night between the husband and wife.

CD. Thanks to the passion of women, the finest man in the world must be either a husband or a lover, either dissolute or impotent.

CDI. The misalliance of two hearts is the worst of all.

CDII. To be loved is not everything; we must insist on appreciation also: and this is only possible from persons of similar quality to ourselves. It follows that love cannot exist, or at least cannot endure, between beings too markedly unequal; nor does this result from the vanity of the superior, but from his proper pride—an instinct of which it would be absurd and impossible to deprive humanity. Vanity is only entertained by weak and vitiated natures, but pride is, past question, a necessary attribute of each well-ordered character.

CDIII. Women only give to friendship what they borrow from love.

CDIV. When an ugly and imperious woman would find favour with the other sex, she is a beggar insisting upon charity.

CDV. A lover too well beloved soon loves his mistress less, and *vice versa.* Is it in love as with other favours, that when we despair of repaying we lose our gratitude?

CDVI. The woman who values her qualities of mind and soul more than her beauty is superior to her sex. The woman who values her beauty more than her qualities of mind and soul is of her sex. But the woman who values her birth and position more than her beauty is at once outside and below her sex.

CDVII. It appears that women have one less section in their brains than men, and one more fibre in their hearts. They need a special organisation to enable them to caress, to care for, and to put up with children.

CDVIII. Nature has entrusted the conservation of all beings to maternal love, and has set it in exquisite, inseparable pleasures and pains, that mothers may not lack their recompense.

CDIX. All is true and all is false in love; love is the only thing about which it is impossible to say anything absurd.

CDX. A lover who pities a reasonable being reminds me of a man who reads fairy tales and banters another because he is reading history.

CDXI. Love is an adventure in a stormy market, and invariably leads to bankruptcy; and it is the bankrupt who gathers the dishonour.

CDXII. One of the best reasons for not marrying is that a man is never entirely a woman's dupe, and a woman never utterly a man's.

CDXIII. Have you ever known a woman who, seeing some male friend of hers cultivating another woman, has believed that the other woman can be unkind? Such is the opinion they have of each other. Draw your own conclusions.

CDXIV. There is no bad thought that man can have of woman, without all women having a worse.

CDXV. Some men have all that is needed to lift them above those petty considerations which thrust mankind below its proper merit, and yet marriage or relations with women have placed them on a level with those who are by no means on a level with them. Wedded life or gallantry serves as a conduit for the smaller passions.

CDXVI. I have known men and women in Society who do not ask sentiment for sentiment, but act for act; and would call off the latter bargain if it seemed likely to lead to the former.

CHAPTER VII.

OF WISE MEN AND MEN OF LETTERS

CDXVII. There is a kind of vehement energy, the inevitable mother or companion of a certain type of talent, which usually condemns its possessors to the misfortune, not of being actually without moral sense or having no admirable instincts, but of yielding constantly to faults which would seem to imply the absence of all morality. They are not masters of their consuming fierceness, and it renders them detestable. It is distressing to think that even when Pope and Swift in England, and Voltaire and Rousseau in France, are judged without jealousy and hatred, and even equitably and kindly, on the attested and admitted evidence of their friends and admirers, they may still be accused and convicted of most reprehensible actions and also, at times, of the most perverse sentiments. *O altitudo!*

CDXVIII. It has been made a subject for remark that writers on Natural History, Physics, Physiology, and Chemistry, are usually men of mild and equable character, and of a happy disposition; while writers on Law and Politics, and even on Moral Philosophy, are of a dismal and melancholy temper. The reason is not far to seek: the former consider Nature and survey the work of the great Being, while the latter observe Society and meditate upon the works of man. Their studies are bound to effect them differently.

CDXIX. If we justly examine the combination of unusual mental and spiritual qualities necessary to a fine discernment and appreciation of good poetry: the touch and delicacy of ear and understanding: we shall soon be satisfied that poets can have even fewer competent judges of their work than geometricians, in spite of the pretension of all classes to connoiseurship. Those poets, therefore, who count the public as nothing and are only concerned with capable critics, should do with their books what the famous mathematician, Viète, did with his, at a time when the study of mathematics was less fashionable than it is today. He only printed a very few copies of his works, for distribution among such as might understand, and be entertained or assisted by them: to the rest of the public he gave no thought at all. But Viète was rich and most poets are poor; besides, a geometrician either has less vanity than a poet or estimates it better.

CDXX. There are men in whom *wit*, that universal instrument, is but a *talent*. They seem to dominate their fellows by it, but it they cannot dominate, for it will not obey the orders of their reason.

CDXXI. I would say of metaphysicians what Scaliger said of the Basques: they are supposed to understand each other, but I do not believe it.

CDXXII. Has a Philosopher, whose inducement is conceit, any right to despise the Courtier, whose motive is gain? It seems to me that the latter carries off the golden coins, while the former is content to hear the chink of them. Is D'Alembert, whose vanity makes him a courtier of Voltaire, at all better than any courtier of Louis the Fourteenth, whose object was power or pension?

CDXXIII. When a kindly-disposed person covets the petty privilege of pleasing others beside his friends (as do so many men, and authors in particular, whose trade is pleasing), it is clear that he can only be prompted thereto by some self-interest or vanity. His sole choice, therefore, lies between a harlot's or a coquette's part, or if you will the part of a comedian. Only the man who makes himself pleasant in a company because he finds that company amusing can really be said to play an honest part.

CDXXIV. Someone has said that stealing from the Ancients is piracy below the Line, but that borrowing from the Moderns is picking pockets at a street corner.

CDXXV. When verse adds wit to the thought of a man who has ordinarily little enough, he possesses the thing called talent; but when, as often happens, verse kills the wit in the thought of a witty writer, the fact affords proof positive that he is not a poet.

CDXXVI. Most contemporary books seem as if they had been made in one day, from yesterday's reading.

CDXXVII. Good taste, tact, and propriety have more in common than Men of Letters affect to believe. Tact is good taste applied to bearing and conduct, and propriety is good taste applied to conversation.

CDXXVIII. Aristotle wisely lays it down in his Rhetoric that every metaphor founded on analogy must be equally true if it be reversed. Thus, old age has been called life's winter, and if you turn the metaphor round you will find it as apposite: that winter is the old age of the year.

CDXXIX. To become a great figure in Letters, as in Politics, or to leave some sensible mark upon them at the least, one must be born at the right moment and find all prepared.

CDXXX. Great lords and wits seek out each others' company, their instinct being to unite two classes, one of which makes a little more dust than the second and the other a little more noise than the first.

CDXXXI. Men of Letters delight in those whom they amuse, just as travellers delight in those whom they astonish.

CDXXXII. What is a Man of Letters, if he be unsupported by his own character, by the excellence of his friends, and by a competency? Should he so lack this last, at all events, as to find it impossible to live agreeably in that Society to which his talents call him, what other need can he be said to have of his fellows? The only course open to him is to seek out some privacy where he may develop his spirit, his reason, and his nature in tranquillity. Why should he bear the burdens of a social state which denies him each single advantage it bestows on other occupations? More than one man of letters has found a happiness in this exile, when he has been forced to embrace it, which he had vainly sought in any other place. Such a man can say that in refusing him all things the world has given him all things. There are countless occasions for quoting the words of Themistocles: "Alas, we were perishing if we had not perished!"

CDXXXIII. When they have read some conspicuously virtuous book, people will often say: "What a pity that writers give no picture of themselves in what they write; a work of this kind cannot tell us whether the author was really such as he would have us think." This remark is certainly justified on occasion; but I have noticed that it is often made to excuse the reader from doing honour to the virtues reflected in the books of a virtuous writer.

CDXXXIV. An author with genuine taste attempting to appeal to our surfeited public is like a young woman in the centre of a circle of old libertines.

CDXXXV. A little philosophy leads men to underrate scholarship, but much philosophy will teach them to esteem it.

CDXXXVI. A poet's labour—and often the labour of a general author as well—is little profitable to himself, and his guerdon from the public varies between "many thanks" and "go about your business." His reward must lie in self-appreciation, and the process of time.

CDXXXVII. A writer's rest, when he has done good work, wins more respect from the public than a fecund activity in producing average books: just as the silence of a brilliant talker carries more weight than the chatter of a poor one.

CDXXXVIII. The success of countless books depends on the sympathy existing between a witless Author and a witless Public.

CDXXXIX. To see the composition of the *Académie Française* one would expect its motto to be that line of Lucretius:

Certare ingenio, contendere nobilitate.[11]

CDXL. The honour of belonging to the *Académie Française* is like the Cross of Saint-Louis, which one is just as likely to see in shilling taverns as at the suppers of Marly.

CDXLI. The *Académie Française* is like the *Opéra* which keeps itself on extraneous revenue, such as subsidies exacted from provincial comic opera, and charges for going from the pit into the boxes. In the same way, the *Académie* keeps itself by the privileges

[11] "To compete with talent, to struggle for high rank"

it procures for its members. It is like the Cidalise of Gresset:

> *Ayez-la, c'est d'abord, ce que vous lui devez,*
> *Et vous l'estimerez après, si vous pouvez.*[12]

CDXLII. There is something in common between literary, and above all theatrical, reputations and the fortunes which used of old to be made in the West Indies. In the early days it was almost sufficient to reach those islands to return with incalculable riches; but the very vastness of the fortunes thus obtained was prejudicial to those of the following generation, since the exhausted earth could yield no more.

CDXLIII. Most theatrical and literary success in our day is a success of ridicule.

CDXLIV. Philosophy searches out each profitable virtue in Ethics and Politics; Eloquence renders it popular; and Poetry makes it, as it were, proverbial.

CDXLV. An eloquent illogical sophist stands in the same relation to a philosophic orator as a conjuror does to a mathematician, Pinetti to Archimedes.

CDXLVI. A man is not necessarily intelligent because he has plenty of ideas, any more than he is a good general because he has plenty of soldiers.

---

[12] "Have it first, that's your obligation
You will value it later, if you can"

CDXLVII. Men of Letters are often censured for retiring from the world. People want them to take an interest *in* Society, even when they can take nothing *out* of her; expect them, in fact, to be eternally present at a lottery in which they hold no ticket.

CDXLVIII. What I admire in the ancient philosophers is their desire to make their lives conform to their writings, a trait which we notice in Plato, Theophrastus and many others. Practical morality was so truly their philosophy's essence that many, such as Xenocrates, Polemon, and Speusippus, were placed at the head of schools although they had written nothing at all. Socrates was none the less the foremost philosopher of his age, although he had not composed a single book or studied any other science than ethics.

CDXLIX. The things we know best are: first what we have divined, then what our experience of men and things has taught us, then the reflections induced by our reading (that is to say not from books but because of books), and lastly what we have been told in books or by our masters.

CDL. Men of Letters, and especially Poets, are like peacocks. We throw a few occasional meagre grains into their cage, and sometimes have them out to see them spread their tails.... But the cocks and hens and ducks and turkeys wander free in the yard, and stuff their crops as much as they please.

CDLI. Successes breed successes, just as money breeds money.

CDLII. There are some books which the most intelligent man in the world cannot write without jobbing a carriage, without going a round of consultation, that is, to men and things, and libraries and manuscripts.

CDLIII. It is almost impossible for Philosophers and Poets not to hate mankind. Firstly, because their taste and talent leads them to the observation of Society, always a heartbreaking enterprise; and, secondly, because the Society on which they exercise that talent hardly ever rewards it (indeed it is lucky to escape unpunished), and this woeful fact is enough to redouble their tendency to sadness.

CDLIV. The Memoirs which even the most seemingly modest Government Officials and Men of Letters have left behind to furnish a history of their lives, betray a secret vanity and remind us of that saint who left a hundred thousand crowns to pay the expenses of his canonisation.

CDLV. It is a grave misfortune when our character loses those rights for us over Society, which our talent has given us.

CDLVI. Great men have produced their greatest work after the age of passion; so is the earth more fertile after volcanoes.

CDLVII. The vanity of worldlings takes clever advantage of the vanity of Men of Letters; for these last have made more than one reputation which has led to high office. At first it is a matter of windy nothings upon either side; but with these the skilful intriguer can swell the sails of his fortune.

CDLVIII. Political Economists are surgeons with excellent scalpels and blunted bistouries; they work on the dead to a marvel and torture the living.

CDLIX. Men of Letters very seldom feel jealous of the exaggerated reputation which books written by men about the Court sometimes acquire; they regard these successes as decent women regard the triumphs of *misses.*

CDLX. The Theatre either confirms or changes the manners of the day; it must, in the nature of things, either chastise or propagate folly. In France we have seen the two systems working alternately.

CDLXI. Many authors think that they love glory when they only love vanity. The two things are very different and even mutually opposed; for the first is a great, and the second a little passion. There is the same difference between vanity and glory as between a coxcomb and a lover.

CDLXII. Posterity judges Men of Letters by their work and not by their position. *What they did, not what they were*, would seem to be Posterity's motto.

CDLXIII. Sperone Speroni very well explains how an author's expression may be limpidly clear to himself and yet obscure to his reader: the reader, he says, is working from expression to thought, and the author from thought to expression.

CDLXIV. The books an author writes with enjoyment are often his best, just as a love child is the handsomest.

CDLXV. In the Fine Arts, and even in other matters, it is only what we have not been taught that we know really well.

CDLXVI. The painter gives soul to a face, and the poet gives a face to a feeling or an idea.

CDLXVII. When La Fontaine's work is bad it is through carelessness, when La Motte's is bad it is through over-subtlety.

CDLXVIII. Perfection in writing a comedy of character is attained by so arranging the intrigue that it could not possibly serve for any other play. Perhaps in all the drama only *Tartuffe* can be said to fulfil this condition.

CDLXIX. Here is an entertaining proof that French philosophers are the worst citizens in the world: they print a great many truths essential to political and economic prosperity, and give a great deal of useful advice in their books; then nearly all the sovereigns of Europe, with the exception of France, follow their teaching; then the prosperity of foreign nations increases, while France remains where she was; then France, by retaining all her old abuses, sinks to a condition of inferiority: this is the fault of the French philosophers. In the same connection, we recall the answer of the Duke of Tuscany to a Frenchman who congratulated him on the felicitous changes he had effected in his States. "You give too much of your praise to me," he said, "for I have taken all my ideas from your French books."

CDLXX. In one of the principal churches of Antwerp I saw the tomb of the celebrated printer, Plantin, decorated to his memory with superb paintings by Rubens. And, so seeing, I recalled how the two Estiennes, Henri and Robert, whose Greek and Latin scholarship rendered the greatest service to the world of letters, dragged out a miserable old age in France, and how Charles Estienne, their successor, died in hospital, when he had contributed almost as much as they to the advancement of learning. I recalled that poverty drove André Duchêne, the father of French history, from Paris to the refuge of his little Champagne farm, and how he died through falling off the top of a cart piled to an enormous height with hay. Adrien de Valois, the first historian of metals, met with a scarcely better fate, and Samson, the father of geography, went on foot, up to the age of seventy, to give lessons for his daily bread. Everyone knows the fate of Du Ryer, Tristan, Maynard, and so many others. Corneille wanted for soup during his last illness, and La Fontaine fared but very little better. If Racine,

Boileau, Molière, and Quinault were more fortunate, it was because their talents were more especially devoted to the King. The Abbé de Longuerue, who has told and collected many such anecdotes of the evil destiny attending illustrious Men of Letters in France, says in conclusion: "Such has always been our custom in this wretched country!" That famous catalogue, prepared for the King and presented to Colbert, of Men of Letters whom His Majesty might desire to pension, was the work of Chapelain, Perrault, Tallemant, and the Abbé Gallois; and these left out such of their colleagues as they personally disliked, and substituted the names of several foreign scholars. They knew full well that both King and Minister would be the more flattered to receive praise which rose four hundred leagues away from Paris.

CHAPTER VIII.

OF SLAVERY AND LIBERTY

OF FRANCE BEFORE AND AFTER THE REVOLUTION

CDLXXI. Those who have spoken enthusiastically of the savage as opposed to the social state, have been laughed to scorn; and yet I would like to know what answer can be made to these three objections: no instance has been found among savages of a madman, a suicide, or a man who has pined for a social existence. On the other hand, a great number of Europeans, at the Cape and in North and South America, who have rejoined their compatriots after living among the natives, have finally reverted to the woods. Now let any who would answer this argument do so without sophistry or verbiage.

CDLXXII. The drawback to Humanity on its social side is that, although the definition *evil is that which harms* is, ethically and politically, sound enough, the statement that *good is that which helps* is quite untrustworthy; since the moment's good may be for long or eternally harmful.

CDLXXIII. When we consider that the only result of the labour and light of thirty or forty centuries has been to deliver three hundred million men, all over the earth, into the grip of some thirty despots; when we consider that these despots are mostly ignorant and imbecile, and that each is governed by three or four knaves who are mostly stupid, what must we think of Humanity, or hope for her future?

CDLXXIV. Nearly all History is a procession of horrors; but, although tyrants hate History in their own lifetime, a general transmission of such crimes is not unpleasing to their descendants, for it distracts attention from their own. History is the only consolation left to the peoples, for it teaches them that their ancestors were as unhappy as themselves, or more unhappy.

CDLXXV. The normal French character is a blend of monkey and setter. It is frolicsome, comical, and fundamentally mischievous like the monkey; and, like the low-bred sporting dog, it fawns and licks its master's hand when it is beaten; it lets itself be put on the chain, and then leaps about in ecstacy when it is loosed for the chase.

CDLXXVI. The Royal Treasure used to be called the Savings. But I suppose people learned to blush at the lie contained in that name, when they saw the wealth of the State so prodigally squandered, for now it is simply called the Royal Treasure.

CDLXXVII. The French Nobility's highest title to respect is its direct descent from those thirty thousand helmeted, cuirassed, bracered, and thigh-pieced persons who rode upon horses armoured in iron and trampled eight or nine million of the real Nation's naked ancestors under their feet. What a wonderful claim to the love and respect of their descendants! And to give a finishing touch to the respectability of this Class, it is renewed and recruited from those who have grown rich by robbing the cottages of the poor who are in no state to pay their impositions. O wretched institutions of Humanity, shaped to inspire all horror and contempt, and yet demanding our respect and reverence!

CDLXXVIII. To require a man to be a gentleman before he can be a ship's captain, is as logical as requiring him to be a King's Secretary before he is fit for foremast-hand or cabinboy.

CDLXXIX. That none may reach a high position in the State unless he be a gentleman is the most fatal of all absurd ideas, and one which is acted upon in nearly every country. It is as if asses should forbid horses all participation in tilts and tournaments.

CDLXXX. Nature does not go to consult Chérin when she would make a saint or a genius.

CDLXXXI. What does it matter if Titus or Tiberius be on the throne when every minister is a Sejanus?

CDLXXXII. If such an historian as Tacitus had written the chronicle of our nobler kings, making an exact statement of all those tyrannical actions and abuses of authority which are now for the most part buried in deep darkness, few of their reigns would inspire less horror than that of Tiberius.

CDLXXXIII. WE may say that there was no more civil government in Rome after the death of

Tiberius Gracchus; when Scipio Nasica left the Senate to go about his deed of violence against the Tribune, he taught the Romans that force alone would make laws in the Forum from that time forth. He was before Sulla in bringing this deadly mystery to light.

CDLXXXIV. The strong secondary interest we feel in reading Tacitus lies in the continual and ever novel contrast between the miserable slaves he sketches for us and the old Republican liberty: between the characters of such as Scaurus and Scipio and the baseness of their descendants. In fact the most effective aspect of Tacitus is Livy.

CDLXXXV. Kings and priests have proscribed the doctrine of suicide to make certain that we escape nothing of our slavery. They wish the dungeon in which we are cast to have no issue; they are like that villain in Dante who walled up the door of the wretched Ugolino's prison.

CDLXXXVI. We write books on Princes' interest, and speak of studying the interest of Princes; has any one ever spoken of studying the interest of the people?

CDLXXXVII. Only the history of free peoples is worth our attention; the history of men under a despotism is merely a collection of anecdotes.

CDLXXXVIII. The real Turkey in Europe is France. In twenty different English writers you will find the phrase: "Despotic countries such as France and Turkey ..."

CDLXXXIX. Ministers are nothing but stewards, and are only important because the estate of the gentleman they serve is very large.

CDXC. A minister often strengthens his own position by making his master commit more and more evils and follies to the detriment of the people; one would say that this kind of complicity binds them more closely together.

CDXCI. Why does a minister in France remain in power in spite of a hundred evil actions? And why is he always dismissed for a single good one?

CDXCII. Who could have supposed that some people would be led to support despotism through their belief in the necessity of encouraging the Arts? It is almost incredible to what an extent the brilliance of Louis the Fourteenth's reign has multiplied the number of those who think along these lines. According to them the final object of Society is to have great tragedies and fine comedies. They would forgive every evil done by the priesthood on the ground that, without priests, there would be no *Tartuffe.*

CDXCIII. Merit and repute give a man no more right to office in France than winning *the rose* [13]gives a village girl the right to be presented at Court.

CDXCIV. France is that place where it is always useful to expose your vices and always dangerous to expose your virtues.

CDXCV. Paris is a singular country where it costs thirty sous to dine, four francs to take the air, a hundred louis for the superfluous adjuncts of the necessary, and four hundred louis if we would have the latter without the former.

CDXCVI. Paris: a city of pleasures and amusements where four-fifths of the people die of grief.

CDXCVII. The phrase which Saint Theresa used to describe Hell is equally applicable to Paris: *A place that stinks, and where there is no love.*

CDXCVIII. It is remarkable that there should be such a multitude of formalities in a Nation as lively and joyous as ours; and the pedantic gravity of our public assemblies is just as astonishing. It almost looks as if the French legislature intentionally acted as a counterpoise to the French citizen.

CDXCIX. It is an established fact that, at the time of Monsieur de Guibert's appointment as governor

---

[13] *Le chapeau de rosière.* The rosière is the rose-queen, or winner of the rose, as the best behaved girl in her village.

of the *Invalides*, there were six hundred so-called soldiers there, who had never been wounded in any way, and who, in practically every instance, had never taken part in a siege or battle. Their service had been as coachmen or lackeys to Lords and Government Officials. Here is a text and matter for reflection!

D. In France we harry the man who rings the alarm bell, and leave the man in peace who starts the fire.

DI. Nearly all women, who live at Versailles or have some little consideration in Paris, are only bourgeois of quality: Mesdames Macquart, presented or unpresented.

DII. There is no longer a French public or a French Nation, for the same reason that lint is not linen.

DIII. The public is governed as it reasons; its own prerogative is foolish speech and that of its governors is foolish action.

DIV. When some public absurdity takes place, I think of the few strangers who may be in Paris at the time, and am ready to weep, for I still love my country.

DV. The English are the only nation which has found out how to limit the power of people who have their faces on half-crowns.

DVI. How is it that, even under the vilest despotism, the race can bear to continue? It is because Nature has sweeter and more imperious laws than any tyrant; because, whether Domitian or Titus reigns, a babe will smile at its mother.

DVII. A philosopher once said: I cannot understand how any Frenchman who has been but a single time into the King's antechamber or the Œil-de-bœuf, can ever say of anyone at all: *He's a great lord.*

DVIII. The flatterers of Princes say that the hunt is an image of war, and perhaps the peasants, whose fields are left desolate, may think the same.

DIX. It is unfortunate for man, but fortunate perhaps for Princes, that the poor and pitiful have not the same pride or instinct as the elephant, which will not propagate its kind when in captivity.

DX. Two things are to be especially noted in the unending struggle which Society allows between the rich and the poor, the noble and the plebeian, the influential and the unknown man. In the first place the actions and words of the two combatants are judged by quite different weights and measures, those of the one against a pound weight, let us say, and those of the other against ten or a hundred. The fact that this disproportion is an admitted one and that we start from it as from a fixed point, is really horrible; that such a standard of acceptance should be sanctioned by law and custom is one of Society's most startling vices, and in itself enough to explain the rest. In the second place it will be noticed that, beyond this initial inequality, there is a further criminal lack of justice: the poor man's pound and the plebeian's is speedily reduced to a quarter of its weight, while ten are added to the rich man's or the noble's hundred, and a hundred to his thousand. This is the natural and inevitable effect of their respective positions; for the first have all their kind to envy them, while the second find props and accomplices in their own few friends, who hope to share in the profits or win a like advantage for themselves.

DXI. It is an incontestable fact that France contains seven million men in need of alms, and twelve million incapable of giving them.

DXII. The Nobility, its members say, is an intermediary between the King and the People. ... Exactly, just as hounds are intermediary between men and hares.

DXIII. What is a Cardinal? A priest who dresses in red and gets a hundred thousand crowns from the King for flouting him in the name of the Pope.

DXIV. The majority of social institutions would seem designed to keep mankind in a state of mental mediocrity, as better fitting him to govern or be governed.

DXV. A citizen of Virginia, who possesses fifty acres of fertile land, pays the equivalent of forty-two sous in our money to enjoy it in peace, under just and benignant laws, with government protection, with security assured to his property and person, with civil and religious liberty, with the right to vote at elections, to be a member of Congress, and, possibly, in course of time, a legislator. But a French peasant of the same standing, in Limousin or the Auvergne, has to submit to tailage, twentieths, and every kind of crushing imposition, for the privilege of being insulted at the caprice of a subdelegate and arbitrarily imprisoned, and for the right to bequeath to his plundered family this wretched and degrading heritage.

DXVI. North America is the one place in the world where the rights of man are fully understood; for the Americans are fitting descendants of those famous republicans who left their country to escape the tyrant. They are a breed of men who have proved themselves worthy to fight and conquer even the English, during a time when the latter had regained their liberty and framed the finest constitution that has ever been. The American revolution will be useful to England herself, for it will force her to re-examine her constitution and weed it of abuses. What will happen then? Being driven out of the continent of North America, the English will throw themselves on the French and Spanish possessions in the West Indies and give them English government, which is founded upon, and even tends to increase, man's natural love of liberty. Then new constitutions will be framed upon a basis of freedom, in the quondam French and Spanish islands, and especially in Spanish America; and thus the English will achieve the signal honour of having given birth to almost the only free countries in the world: the only peoples who will have known and preserved the rights of man, and therefore the sole ones actually worthy to bear his name. But how many years will be needed to make this revolution operative? Enormous stretches of land will have to be cleansed of the French and Spanish, who would only perpetuate slavery, and colonised with Englishmen, bearing the seeds of freedom. These seeds will germinate, and at last bring forth that final revolution which will drive the English themselves from the two Americas and all the Indies.

DXVII. An Englishman respects the law and rejects or despises authority; a Frenchman respects authority and despises the law. The latter must be taught to reverse his opinion; but perhaps this is impossible in the present state of the Nation's ignorance: an ignorance which must not be denied on the strength of the enlightenment which has spread in the principal cities.

DXVIII. I am all and the rest are nothing: there you have Despotism, Aristocracy, and *their* adherents. I am another, another is I: there you have popular government and *its* adherents. Now take your choice.

DXIX. All who come forth from the people take arms for the oppression of their class, from the militiaman, and the lawyer who becomes a King's Secretary, to the preacher who leaves his village to urge submission to an arbitrary power, and the bourgeois' son who takes up historiography. It is the tale of the soldiers of Cadmus over again; the armies in front turn round and attack their brothers.

DXX. The poor are the negroes of Europe.

DXXI. As animals perish when they breathe the air above a certain height, a slave dies in the atmosphere of liberty.

DXXII. People are governed with the head; kindness of heart is little use in chess.

DXXIII. Bacon says that human understanding ought to be begun all over again: so should human Society.

DXXIV. You can lessen the People's ferocity by lessening their ills, as surely as you can cure their maladies with soup.

DXXV. I notice that phenomenal men who have performed some revolutionary action seemingly through sheer genius, have often been seconded by the spirit of their time and most auspicious circumstances. We know of the attempts which had been made before the great voyage of Vasco de Gama to the West Indies; and it is common knowledge that many navigators were convinced of the existence of great islands in the West, and very probably a continent, before Colombus discovered America. We are also aware that Columbus himself possessed the papers of a celebrated pilot with whom he had been in treaty. Philip had prepared everything for the Persian war before his death. And there were several heretical sects in revolt against the abuses of the Roman Communion before Luther and Calvin, and even before Wyclif.

DXXVI. It is commonly believed that Peter the Great woke up one morning with the idea of a universal Russian re-birth; but even M. de Voltaire admits that it was Peter's father, Alexis, who first formed the plan of importing the arts into that country. There is a maturity to be awaited in all things, and happy is the man who coincides with it!

DXXVII. The National Assembly of 1789 gave the French people a constitution stronger than themselves; its business now is to raise the Country by good public education to the level of its government. Our legislators must imitate those skilful physicians who introduce restoratives into an exhausted patient by means of stomachics.

DXXVIII. Considering the great number of deputies to the National Assembly of 1789, and the mass of unreasonable prepossessions which the majority of them entertained, one would have said that they had destroyed prejudice in order to lay their hands upon it, as men might destroy a building to steal the bricks.

DXXIX. One of the reasons why assemblies and bodies of men are scarcely ever capable of other than imbecile action, is that the best thing that could be urged for or against a person or measure cannot be said aloud in public without great danger or inconvenience.

DXXX. The moving chaos must have been more chaotic in that moment when God created the World than when it reposed in peaceable disorder, and the excessive apparent disruption of our Society in its process of reorganisation is somewhat analogous.

DXXXI. Courtiers and others, who used to batten on the monstrous abuses which were crushing France, now say that such things might have been reformed without being destroyed as we destroyed them. They might as well have expected us to cleanse the Augean stables with a feather-duster.

DXXXII. Under the old administration, a philosopher would enunciate a series of daring truths, and straightway some man, who was an office-holder through birth or accident, would read them, and soften down and modify them, and reduce them to a twentieth, and thus gain the reputation of being a dangerous and brilliant person. Then he would temper his zeal and make his fortune, while the philosopher went to the Bastille. But, under the new administration, it is the philosopher who makes his fortune. Instead of leading him to prison and clearing the mind of a fool to acquire office, his ideas will now bring office to himself; and we must imagine how the host of those whom he puts to one side in his progress will enjoy getting used to this novel state of affairs!

DXXXIII. Was it not too delightful to see that the Marquis de Bièvre, a grandson of the surgeon

Maréchal, thought it necessary to escape to England, as Monsieur de Luxembourg and the great aristocrats escaped, after the catastrophe of the Fourteenth of July in 1789?

DXXXIV. Because theologians have always been true to the policy of oppressing and throwing dust into the eyes of men, and because they have ever been the tools of government, they now gratuitously assume that the great majority of mankind is perpetually doomed to that state of stupidity which purely mechanical and manual occupations are apt to induce. They take it for granted that artisans cannot rise to the level of knowledge which will make them value the rights of men as citizens. From this one would imagine such knowledge to be very complicated; but suppose that a quarter of the time and care which has been lavished on brutalising the lower classes had been spent in their enlightenment; suppose that they had been given a catechism containing the first principles of the rights of man and of the duties devolving from those rights, instead of a metaphysical one as absurd as it is unintelligible, we should be astonished to see how far a good elementary text book would have taken the people. Again, suppose that they had preached a gospel of the knowledge of the rights of man and of his duty to defend them, instead of that doctrine of patience, suffering, renunciation, and self-abasement, which is so convenient to the usurper, we would have seen that, when Nature created humanity for a social life, she endowed it with all the good sense necessary to found that social life on reason.

CHAPTER IX.

STRAY OBSERVATIONS

DXXXV. It is a pleasant allegory, Minerva, the goddess of Wisdom, rejecting the flute when she found that it did not become her.

DXXXVI. And another pretty allegory lies in the myth which tells us that true dreams come forth from the gates of horn and false dreams, all pleasant illusions that is, from the gates of ivory.

DXXXVII. A wit said of Monsieur …, an old companion who returned to him in his prosperity: "He not only wants his friends to be fortunate, he insists upon it."

DXXXVIII. A man who began seducing a woman before he was ready, said: "Madame, would it be all the same to you if you retained your virtue for another quarter of an hour?"

DXXXIX. Plutarch says that Love puts all the other passions to silence: Love, in fact, is a dictator in whose presence all other dignitaries faint away.

DXL. On hearing the love of mind for mind inveighed against, because of the harmful properties of imagination, Monsieur … would say: "I personally have no need to fear it. When a woman pleases me and makes me happy, I yield to the feeling she inspires, but reserve the right not to be deceived in her, in case she turns out to be unsuitable. My imagination is the upholsterer whom I send to furnish my apartment when I am satisfied that I shall be properly housed there; if I am not so satisfied, I give no order, and the expense of a memory is spared."

DXLI. Monsieur de L … has told me that, in the very moment of his grief on learning of Madame de B …'s unfaithfulness, he realised that he no longer cared for her, that his love had disappeared for ever. He was as a man who walks in a field and hears the noise of a partridge rising and flying away.

DXLII. You are surprised that Monsieur de L … visits Mme. de D … ? But I believe him to be in love with Madame de B …, my dear Sir, and you know that a woman is often the intermediate shade that reconciles, rather than matches, two vivid and discordant colours.

DXLIII. A clumsy benefactor has been likened to a goat who lets herself be milked and then kicks over the pail.

DXLIV. His imagination gives birth to one illusion in the moment of losing another: it is like that rose tree which blossoms all the year round.

DXLV. Monsieur … declared that he loved peace, silence, and obscurity above all things. *A sick room, in fact*, said someone.

DXLVI. Someone said to Monsieur …, who was a brilliant figure in Society: "You did not make any great expenditure of your wit yesterday evening at So-and-so's." "You must remember the Dutch proverb," answered Monsieur …, "*there can be no economy without small change.*"

DXLVII. A woman is nothing of herself, being only what she appears to the man who pays her attention; that is why she becomes so angry with those who do not see her as she would be seen. They destroy her very existence. Man is less vulnerable, because, even in these circumstances, he remains what he is.

DXLVIII. His nobility led him to take a few steps in the direction of Fortune, and then to despise her.

DXLIX. Monsieur …, who is a confirmed bachelor, remarked that marriage was a state too perfect for imperfect man.

DL. Madame de Fourq …, once said to a lady-companion of hers: "You never know the right things to say to me under particular circumstances. For instance it is all too likely that I shall some day lose my husband and be inconsolable; then you must say …"

DLL Monsieur d'Osmond was gambling in public two or three days after his wife had died in the country. "Surely, d'Osmond," said someone, "it is hardly decent to gamble so soon after your wife's death." "Oh, but I have not yet heard the news officially," answered d'Osmond. "Still it is not right," persisted the other. "But I am playing for such small stakes," d'Osmond replied.

DLII. Diderot used to say that an author *may* have a mistress who composes books, but *must* have a wife who composes shirts.

DLIII. A doctor advised Monsieur de … to have a cautery, but the latter refused, and in the course of a few months recovered his health. Meeting him one day and seeing that he was much better, the doctor asked him what remedy he had used. "None," answered his patient, "I have been living well and having a good time all the Summer; I keep a mistress. But now that Winter is coming I am afraid that my eye trouble may return. Would you not advise me to have a cautery?" "No," replied the doctor gravely, "you have a mistress, and that is enough. It might be wiser to leave her and be cauterised, but it is not absolutely necessary. At any rate one cautery is sufficient."

DLIV. A man who cared nothing for life, murmured as he died: "This will be a sell for Doctor Bouvard."

DLV. The tyranny of fashion is a curious thing. Monsieur de la Trémoille, who lived apart from his wife and neither loved nor respected her, heard that she was sick of the smallpox. He shut himself in with her, caught the same disease, died of it, and left her a vast fortune with permission to marry again.

DLVI. There is a kind of harmful modesty which is the result of ignorance, and sometimes affects men of superior character to their hurt by keeping them in a state of apparent mediocrity. I am reminded of the remark that a certain gentleman of acknowledged eminence once made at luncheon to some persons about the Court: "I regret the time it has taken me, gentlemen, to realise my vast superiority to you."

DLVII. Conquerors are always considered as the first of men, just as the lion is always called the king of beasts.

DLVTII. After his journey in Sicily, Monsieur … argued against the popular impression that the interior of those parts is infested by brigands. He said that wherever he went he was told that the robbers were somewhere else. "Ah, they would not tell you that in Paris," answered Monsieur de B…, that pleasant misanthrope.

DLIX. We are well aware that there are Parisian thieves known to, and almost acknowledged by, the police; if they are not actual informers they at least obey constabulary discipline. One day the Lieutenant of Police sent for some of these men: "Such-and-such was stolen on so-and-so in such-and-such a quarter." "At what time, Monsieur?" "At two in the afternoon." "It was not we, then, Monsieur; we cannot accept responsibility; it must have been stolen by *strangers.*"

DLX. Pope says that the poets keep the critics and journalists in daily bread: just, added Monsieur …, as every honest man in Paris feeds the police-spy.

DLXI. He was passionate and thought he was wise; I was a fool and suspected it; I was the nearer to wisdom.

DLXII. There is an excellent Turkish proverb: "I give thanks unto thee, O Misfortune, if thou hast journeyed alone."

DLXIII. The Italians say: *Sotto umbilico ne religione ne verita.*[14]

DLXIV. As a justification of Providence, Saint Augustine says that it leaves the evil man upon earth that he may become good, or make the good man better.

DLXV. Mankind is so perverse that even to hope, even to desire to amend him, and make him reasonable and honest, is an absurdity, a romantic foible not to be pardoned except in simple youth.

DLXVI. "I have utterly lost my taste for mankind," said Monsieur de L … "Then you have not lost your taste," said Monsieur de N …

DLXVII. Monsieur …, a disillusioned old man, once said to me: "The remainder of my life is a half-sucked orange and I do not know why I squeeze it, for the juice is certainly not worth the effort."

[14] "Below the navel, neither religion nor truth"

DLXVIII. Our language is supposed to be the friend of clarity. If that is so, says Monsieur …, it is because we love what most we need; for our language is always ready to fall into obscurity unless it be skilfully handled.

DLXIX. The Poet, the man of imagination, must believe in God:

Ab Jove principium musis,
or *Ab Jove Musarum primordia.*[15]

DLXX. Monsieur … used to say that verses, like olives, are better for being kept in the pocket.

DLXXI. Foolish, ignorant, and vicious persons go to books for their thoughts and judgment, and for all their elevated and noble sentiments, just as a rich woman goes with her money to a draper.

DLXXII. Monsieur … says that scholars pave the temple of Glory.

DLXXIII. Monsieur … is a true Greek pedant to whom every modern fact recalls an ancient instance. If you speak to him of the Abbé Terray, he at once cites Aristides, Controller-General of the Athenians.

DLXXIV. When a Man of Letters was offered the whole of the *Mercure* at three sous a volume, he said: "I will wait till it is marked down."

---

[15] "From Jove the beginning of the Muses" or "What belongs to the Muses begins with Jove"

DLXXV. Monsieur de …, a once passionate lover, was twitted by his friends on his premature old age, because he had lived for several years in continence. "You are inapt," he answered, "I was very old a few years ago, but now I am very young."

DLXXVI. Most benefactors are like unskilful generals who take the city and leave the citadel intact.

DLXXVII. A wit, who saw that he was being mischievously quizzed by a couple of wags, said: "You are mistaken, gentlemen, I am neither a fool nor a dolt, but somewhat between the two."

DLXXVIII. An ugly woman who dresses up when she must sit in company with young and pretty ones, is doing, in her own way, what a man does who cannot abide to be beaten in argument: skilfully changing the point at issue. She tries to shift the question from *who is the fairest* to *who is the richest.*

DLXXIX. When Monsieur D … repulsed the advances of a beautiful woman, her husband conceived as great a hatred for him as if he had accepted them. "Good God, if he only knew how funny he was," said Monsieur B …, and people laughed at this.

DLXXX. A man who had been notoriously blind to his wife's misconduct and had even many times connived at it for his own advantage, showed utter desolation when she died, and said to me quite seriously: "I can use Louis the Sixteenth's words on the death of Marie-Thérèse: 'This is the first time she has ever grieved me.'"

DLXXXI. A beautiful woman whose lover had a sullen and married air once said to him: "When you are seen in Society with my husband, Monsieur, you are expected to be more genial than he is."

DLXXXII. A doctor used to say: "Only heirs pay really well."

DLXXXIII. There is such a thing as low gratitude.

DLXXXIV. In cities the old are more corrupt than the young; rottenness follows maturity.

DLXXXV. There is no virtue poverty cannot spoil. It is not the cat's fault that she takes the servant's dinner.

DLXXXVI. Monsieur D … L … explained to Monsieur D … how he had been vilely treated in a certain matter, and asked him: "What would you do in my place?" The other, who was an egoist because he hated mankind, and had become indifferent to injustice because he had suffered so much of it, answered him coldly: "In your place, Monsieur, I would look after my stomach and keep my tongue red."

DLXXXVII. A doctor of the Sorbonne said in his rage against the *Système de la Nature:* "It is an execrable, an abominable book; it *proves* atheism."

DLXXXVIII. It is with philosophy as with monasticism. Many take the vows in spite of themselves, and rage for the rest of their lives; some learn patience, and a few even grow happy and silent and do not try to proselytize; but those who are in despair at their own enlistment *seek to recruit novices.*

DLXXXIX. Some people put their books into their library, but Monsieur … puts his library into his books.

DXC. A little girl said to Monsieur …, the author of a book on Italy: "Monsieur, you have written a book about Italy?" "Yes, Mademoiselle." "Have you been there?" "Indeed I have." "Did you write your book after you went, or before you went?"

DXCI. Monsieur …, who was often asked to read his poems and very much disliked doing so, admitted that whenever he began his reading he used to think of a certain mountebank on the Pont Neuf. This fellow always said to his monkey as it began its tricks: "We are not here to amuse ourselves, my dear Bertrand, we are here to please the honourable company."

DXCII. There is a kind of melancholy which amounts to spiritual greatness.

DXCIII. A country priest, in asking for the prayers of his congregation, said: "Gentlemen, pray to God for the soul of the owner of the chateau, who has died of his wounds in Paris." (He had been a libertine.)

DXCIV. They say that Monsieur ..., as he adds to the number of vile services he does for a great lord, becomes progressively more attached to him, just as the ivy clings the closer by creeping.

DXCV. A very rich man said of the poor: "It is no use not giving them anything, the extraordinary fellows always go on asking." More than one Prince might say the same of his courtiers.

DXCVI. A provincial worried his neighbour with questions at the King's Mass. "Who is that lady?" "The Queen." "And that?" "Madame." "And that?" "The Comtesse d'Artois." "And that?" "The late queen," answered the Versailles man irritably.

DXCVII. At the time of the *Assemblée des Notables* (1787), when the question was raised of granting considerable powers to intendants in provincial assemblies, a certain influential personage showed himself favourable to the motion. A subtle friend of his was approached on the matter and promised to make him change his opinion. He succeeded, and when he was asked how, he answered: "He is absolutely infatuated on the subject of birth, so I did not insist upon the intendants' tyrannical abuse of their power, but told him that some exceedingly wellborn gentlemen had to call them: *Monseigneur.* He saw the enormity of this, and it brought him round to your opinion."

DXCVIII. Definition of a despotic government: A state in which the superior is vile and the inferior is vilified.

DXCIX. Ministers have brought about the destruction of kingly authority, just as priests have undermined the authority of religion. God and the King have suffered from the stupidity of their valets.

DC. A man said innocently to one of his friends: "We condemned three men to death this morning. Two of them certainly deserved it."

Fin

www.ingramcontent.com/pod-product-compliance
Lightning Source LLC
Chambersburg PA
CBHW071936190726
48293CB00004B/1268

* 9 7 8 1 9 5 4 3 5 7 3 6 5 *